# Retail
# Category
# Management

# Deborah C. Fowler
Texas Tech University

# Ben K. Goh
Texas Tech University

**Prentice Hall**

Boston   Columbus   Indianapolis   New York   San Francisco   Upper Saddle River
Amsterdam   Cape Town   Delhi   Dubai   Hong Kong   London   Madrid   Mexico City   Milan
Montreal   Munich   Paris   Sao Paulo   Seoul   Singapore   Sydney   Taipei   Tokyo   Toronto

**Editorial Director:** Vernon R. Anthony
**Acquisitions Editor:** Sara Eilert
**Editorial Assistant:** Doug Greive
**Director of Marketing:** David Gesell
**Senior Marketing Manager:** Harper Coles
**Senior Marketing Coordinator:** Alicia Wozniak
**Senior Marketing Assistant:** Les Roberts
**Project Manager:** Holly Shufeldt
**Senior Art Director:** Jayne Conte
**Cover Designer:** Suzanne Behnke
**Cover Art:** Shutterstock
**Full-Service Project Management/Composition:** Mohinder Singh/Aptara®, Inc.
**Printer/Binder:** Courier/Kendallville
**Cover Printer:** Lehigh-Phoenix Color
**Text Font:** HelveticaNeue-Light

**Chapter Opening Photo Credits:** Dmitry Fisher/Shutterstock, p. 2; Vasina Nazarenko/Fotolia, LLC - Royalty Free, p. 14; Dmitry Fisher/Shutterstock, p. 26; Andris Piebalgs/Fotolia, LLC - Royalty Free, p. 38; Tatiana Popova/Shutterstock, p. 50; AZ/Shutterstock, p. 62; AZ/Shutterstock, p. 74; Zibedik/Shutterstock, p. 84; Galina Barskaya/Shutterstock, p. 96; Alice/Shutterstock, p. 108

Credits and acknowledgments borrowed from other sources and reproduced, with permission, in this textbook appear on appropriate page within text.

**Library of Congress Cataloging-in-Publication Data**
Fowler, Deborah C.
   Retail category management / Deborah C. Fowler, Ben K. Goh. — 1st ed.
      p. cm.
   Includes bibliographical references and index.
   ISBN-13: 978-0-13-515208-9
   ISBN-10: 0-13-515208-9
   1. Retail trade—Management. 2. Marketing. 3. Consumers. I. Goh, Ben K.   II. Title.
HF5429.F65 2012
658.8'7—dc22

                                        2010046571

10 9 8 7 6 5 4 3 2
**Prentice Hall**
is an imprint of

www.pearsonhighered.com

ISBN 10:      0-13-515208-9
ISBN 13: 978-0-13-515208-9

*We dedicate this book to our families who have supported us throughout our careers: Bob and Libby Fowler and the entire Goh family.*

Retailing is a constantly changing environment, and the use of technology can help improve customer service, profitability, and assortment planning. One facet of the use of technology is through category management. Category management began as a project to help grocery retailers project the correct product for the correct store for the correct customer at the correct time in the correct quantities. This textbook is one of the first to offer an in-depth perspective of the concept of category management.

This text seeks to offer this perspective by:

- Presenting 10 chapters, designed to be manageable in either a semester-long course or as a supplement to an introduction to retailing or supply chain management.
- Describes the process, including the original eight-step category management cycle, the new cycle with shopping insights, along with careers in the category management industry.

# Download Instructor Resources from the Instructor Resource Center

To access supplementary materials online, instructors need to request an instructor access code. Go to www.pearsonhighered.com/irc to register for an instructor access code. Within 48 hours of registering, you will receive a confirming e-mail Including an instructor access code. Once you have received your code, locate your text in the online catalog and click on the Instructor Resources button on the left side of the catalog product page. Select a supplement, and a login page will appear. Once you have logged in, you can access instructor material for all Prentice Hall textbooks. If you have any difficulties accessing the site or downloading a supplement, please contact Customer Service at http://247. prenhall.com.

# Acknowledgments

We wish to express our appreciation to the following persons who contributed freely of their time to make Retail Category Management a better book. Special appreciation goes to:

- Mr. Kevin Stadler, who introduced the concept of category management to us and provided the JDA Intactix software that made teaching category management a pleasure
- Ms. Karen Storey of JDA, who has always provided us with assistance
- Dr. Brian Harris, the "father of category management," for his insight and for developing the field
- Mr. Jeff Saitow of the Nielsen Company who speaks to our students every semester
- Mr. Winston Weber, the pioneer of category management
- Mr. Dan Desmarais of Cantactix Solutions, Inc., who patiently read and offered advice during the development of the book
- Ms. Donna Frazier, Founding Director of CPG CatNet, the association for Category Development Professionals, for her support of this book at the Retail Management Program at Texas Tech
- JDA, the Supply Chain Company, who provided software and technical support in this endeavor
- The Hartman Group
- Dr. Lynn Huffman and Dr. Shane Blum, past and present chairpersons in the Department of Nutrition, Hospitality, and Retailing

A special thanks to Vern Anthony, Christine Buckendahl, Sara Eilert, Doug Greive, and Jill Jones-Renger. Their belief in this book has been phenomenal, and their patience even more so.

On a personal note, I would like to thank the following:

- My teaching assistants who taught the category management labs and patiently helped me prepare for class: Jill Godfrey, Christina Kayfus Koch, Amy Reed, Megan Smith, Whitney Stagner, and Alyssa Walker
- My teaching assistants who managed my other labs so that I could focus on writing: Eun Kyong "Cindy" Choi, Sang-Mook Lee, and Nathan Stokes

# contents

# Retail
# Category
# Management

# CATEGORY
# MANAGEMENT

**LEARNING GOALS**

On completion of this chapter, the student will be able to:

- Explain the concept of category management.
- Define category management.
- Summarize the guiding principles of category management.
- Define the term **category** and give examples.
- Understand how retailing has evolved to develop category management.
- Discuss technological innovations facilitating category management.
- Contrast brand management and category management.
- Compare the roles of retail buyer, category captain, and category advisor.
- State the core features of category management.

1

# Introduction

A simple way to conceptualize category management is by viewing a retail store as a mall. For example, imagine a mass merchandiser such as Walmart as a mall. Then visualize the different categories in the store, such as soft drinks or pet food, as independent retailers in the mall. Whether the store format is a grocery store, pet store, bookstore, or mass merchandiser, the concept is the same: a group of businesses operating under a single roof with a mall manager. These "stores" all focus on the goal of maximizing profit for their "store" or, in this case, their category. Ultimately, when each "store" or category achieves its profit goal, it logically leads to an increase in profit for the retailer.

Retailers that use category management, such as mall managers, realize that businesses must work together to provide the optimal customer experience by offering the merchandise sought by the customer. Through this collaborative process, retailers and their customers reap the benefits of a focused approach to retail management.

# Category Management Defined

Throughout the years, several definitions have been given to the process of category management. For the purpose of this book, **category management** is defined as the collaboration between **vendors** and retailers to provide optimal service to the customer while providing profit and sales to the retailer and vendors. The most frequently cited definition was developed by the Partnering Group, who defined category management as a retailer/vendor process of managing categories as **strategic business units (SBU)**, producing enhanced business results focused on delivering customer value and profit and sales for entire groups of products, called categories. An SBU is a distinct unit of business with defined strategies, objectives, and competitors for serving an external market (Partnering Group 1995).

The Institute of Grocery Distribution, based in the United Kingdom, defines category management as "the strategic management of product groups through trade partnerships which aims to maximize sales and profit by satisfying consumer and shopper needs" (http://www.igd.com/index.asp?id=1&fid=1&sid=6&tid=38&cid). They identify two key elements: (1) provide customers with what they want, where they want, and when they want; and (2) group products into categories to reflect customers' needs based on the product used, consumed, or purchased (Food and Grocery Information).

In the United States, the Federal Trade Commission (FTC) defines category management as "An organizational approach in which the management of a retail establishment is broken down into categories of like products. Through category management decisions about product selection, placement, promotion and pricing are made on a category-by-category basis with an eye to maximizing the profitability of the category as a whole" (Leary 2004).

Category management offers retailers and their vendors the opportunity to develop high levels of expertise in an area and provide the best merchandise mix for the targeted customer. The primary purpose of this process is to ensure high levels of productivity within each unit or category. Category management allows retailers to improve their product assortment and merchandise mix, lower overall prices, reduce their **out-of-stock (OOS)** situation, and make shopping in the store easier for the customer.

The average increase in sales attributed to category management is about 19 percent for the retailer and 12 percent for manufacturers or vendors, all while minimizing inventory and maximizing space allocation (Cannondale Associates 2007). The reason for the difference in the sales increase percentage between retailers and manufacturers or vendors is because retailers use their space more efficiently by increasing the number of vendors to offer better product assortments. For example, retailers may have reduced shelf space for each vendor to provide additional space for more vendors to increase the merchandising mix. Therefore, the overall sales growth for each vendor is lower than that of the retailer.

# Guiding Principles of Category Management

Through the implementation of category management, categories become profit centers with space allocation aimed at maximizing the value for the customer, while improving the profitability of the category and retailer. To successfully implement category management, retailers often follow three core principles:

1. **Focus of strategic management of a product group.** In the past, retailers planned their stores based on operational convenience. For example, they may have placed all merchandise with a single brand together. With category management the categories are defined according to customer shopping behavior. Categories are defined differently based on the retail type. For instance, in a mass merchandiser all pet supplies may be a single category, whereas in a pet store, the categories are defined differently; they may define cat food and dog food as two separate categories.

2. **Collaboration between retailers and vendors.** Retailers and vendors become **trade partners**. They work together in the pursuit of profit and productivity while providing a desirable level of customer satisfaction. Although each partner has additional goals focused on their brand or retail concept, they realize they need each other to be successful. However, the trade partners must work cooperatively to ensure that all brands are successful. This includes the leading manufacturer's brands, private label brands owned by the retailer, and specialty brands—including regional brands—which all must have adequate representation and opportunity to generate sales and profit. Although retailers are interested in the success of the brands offered, they focus on the overall success of the category.

3. **Satisfying the customers' needs.** Category management must address the customers' shopping preferences, routines, and shopping styles. Merchandise is grouped by categories that address the customers' needs.

# Definition of Category

A **category** is a distinct, manageable group of products or services that customers perceive as related, or as substitutes. For example, baking goods as a category may include cake and brownie mixes. There are many variations in flavor, color, or brand within this category. A category may also be defined by occasion. An example of defining a category by grouping complementary products is the Easter holiday. All products—including candy, baskets, and toys associated with Easter—are placed in a single location.

Categories allow retailers to look at a group of products as a unit. This translates into a more comprehensive analysis of retail data, including **point of sale (POS)** data of retail sales by dollar and unit. In the past retailers and vendors focused on one product at a time. For example, if you focus simply on Tide® detergent you are interested in the sales and profit generated only by Tide. The amount of shelf space allocated to Tide detergent appeared to have a direct relationship to sales and profit. With the change of focus to the category of detergent, all brands of laundry detergent, fabric softeners, and other products within that category—including stain removers and dryer sheets—are of interest. This global approach allows the retailer to ensure that all products within the allocated space are adequately represented. Further, the **planograms** may be adapted to focus on the brands and sizes preferred by the customers shopping at a particular store. A planogram (POG) is a detailed depiction of a display of computer images or a photograph that analyzes data to ensure the success of the category.

Retailers implement category management for many reasons. The two major reasons are to eliminate wasted space and to focus only on the merchandise sought by the customers at a given location, thus increasing the profit margin.

# Evolution of Retailing to Develop Category Management

The concept of category management is not new; the term was coined by Brian Harris in the early 1990s. He is the cofounder of the Partnering Group and considered by many as the father of category management. The original mom-and-pop grocery store serving a small community set the foundations of category management. Small retailers stocked merchandise based on the wants and needs of their clientele. The inventory system was done simply by visually checking the shelves. Customers asked the retailers to order special goods or the retailer anticipated the purchases of the customers and ordered accordingly, in effect practicing micromarketing. With the advent of self-service grocery stores, retailers began to rely on their vendors, distributors, and food brokers to assist in assortment planning. Unfortunately, the micromarketing aspect of the mom-and-pop store was lost with this transition.

# Technological Innovations Facilitating Category Management

Although the principles of category management are not new, the introduction of technological applications designed specifically for inventory management makes it easier for retailers to gather data instantaneously. Technology moved retailers from visually determining the need to restock items to a computer-generated stockkeeping inventory. One of the first innovations was the **Universal Product Code (UPC)**. The UPC is a bar and numeric code that enables retailers and their partners to use technology to maintain and assess inventories. The UPC code also allows retailers to scan the code rather than the retail associates having to manually key in the price of each item. The UPC code not only improved the ability to track stock, but also eventually increased the speed of the check-out procedure.

Other major technological innovations that facilitated the practice of category management were **electronic data interchange (EDI)** and **Quick Response (QR)**. EDI allows retailers and vendors to electronically exchange data, including POS data, usually encoded using the UPC code. EDI provides an electronic pathway for retailers and their vendors to set up criteria for reordering once a minimum stock level is reached. QR is a business strategy for reducing inventory in the pipeline and shortening the cycle time for a product to be made, distributed, and sold. Both EDI and QR strive to provide both retailers and suppliers with current and immediate information regarding supplies and inventory. Technology enabled the process of the category management; however, its implementation is both a human resources issue and a change in the organizational structure.

# Brand Management and Category Management

Another major change in retailing due to the implementation of category management is the shift in focus from **brand management** to category management. In traditional retailing the brand and product were most important sales strategy. Brand management entails the application of marketing techniques to ensure the value of the brand by retaining and acquiring new customers. The value of the brand is determined by the profit generated for the manufacturer through an increase in both sales and prices. Brand management and category management are related, but the perspectives are quite different. In brand management, retailers and vendors focus first on the product or **stockkeeping unit (SKU) gross margin** (retail sales price − cost of a product), then the vendor's gross margin, then the subcategory margin, and finally the margin generated by the category. This triangle of analysis is inverted in category management. The focus is first on the category margin, then the subcategory, the vendor, and finally the gross margin generated by the SKU. Figure 1.1 compares the change in the hierarchy of analysis. In the past retailing focused on the retailer's thought process rather than the customer's behavior and thought process. By inverting the triangle, retailers began to change their way of thinking and to understand the customer's buying behavior and decision-making hierarchy. One way retailers focus on the customer is through the use of **loyalty cards**. Loyalty cards are scanned at the check-out and associate purchases with the individual shopper. In category management the success of the category is most important, then the subcategory, then the vendor, and finally the SKU or product. This change of analysis is crucial to the implementation and success of category management and exemplifies the difference between brand management and category management.

Category management relies on collaboration and cooperation, changing the traditional roles in the retail and vendor organizational structure. The role of the brand manager changes and evolves during the implementation process. According to Wileman and Jary (1997, 132), "the intersection of buying and merchandising and marketing is the heart of retail brand management, and its focus is category management."

**FIGURE 1.1** *Hierarchy of Analysis*

*Source:* Efficient Consumer Response (ECR)—Enhancing Consumer Value in the Grocery Industry, 1993. Reprinted with Permission of the Food Marketing Institute and the Joint Industry Project on ECR.

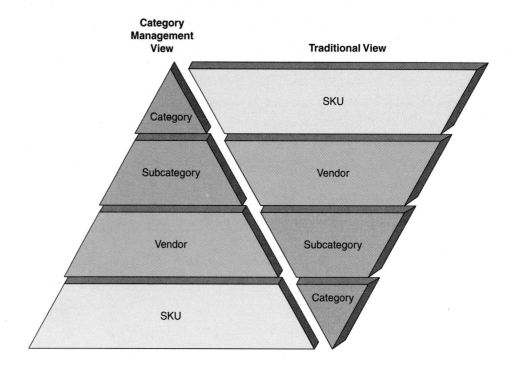

# Category Management Team

As with the change in the role of brand managers, the role of merchandisers and buyers changed with the development of category management. The organizational structure of traditional retailing separated merchandisers and buyers by function and often goals. The buyers purchased the goods; then the merchandisers prepared and planned the method of display. Marketing professionals focused on the way customers shopped, and buyers focused on the products. With category management, a cross-functional team of buyers and merchandisers form a category management team. They develop planograms (graphic or photographic displays of merchandise on shelf space).

The person ultimately responsible for the category is the **category manager**. He or she must achieve the goals—including advertising, promotions, pricing, assortment planning, and merchandising (shelf space allocation and placement)—established by the retailer. Although the category manager and/or category management team may be employed by the retailer or the vendors, regardless of the employer, the role of category manager combines the responsibilities of both the buyer and the merchandiser.

An essential component to the success of the implementation of the category management team is the **category captain**, usually a supplier or vendor appointed by the retailer to be in charge of a particular category. Retailers typically choose a category captain for each category of merchandise in the store. The category captain is usually a team of people that performs the functions of the merchandiser for a particular category, and usually has access to most of the data for that category—including total dollar sales or total unit sales, **market data**, and **syndicated data**—from sources such as ACNielsen. The category captain is responsible for the success of the category development and growth; with this responsibility, the category captain helps the retailer:

1. Define the category.
2. Determine the role the category plays in the assortment mix of the retailer.

3. Evaluate the performance of the category by setting goals and assessing the progress in achieving those goals.
4. Identify the target customer, determine the ideal merchandise mix, and determine the most efficient display of products in the category.
5. Ensure the implementation of the plan.

They may analyze the data to recommend prices and shelf-space allocation of their own products as well as their competitors. One interesting fact about the category captain is that it is often assigned to the **category leader**—the vendor with the largest share in a category. However, some vendors that are category leaders prefer to serve as an advisor in order to reduce their costs.

Another position within the category management team is the **category advisor**. The retailer usually assigns this position to a competitor in the same category. This competitor provides second opinions to the decisions made by the category captain. The category advisor is usually a team of people, often called a **validator**, **co-captain**, or **consultant**; however, their role is the same. They review the planograms and promotions to determine whether the planogram is fair to all vendors within the category and report directly to the retailer. Depending on the philosophy of the retailer, the role of category advisor may be strong or weak depending on the breadth and depth of their decision-making responsibility. Some vendors are too small to afford a category manager. These vendors must rely on category captains, category advisors, and retailers to ensure the fairness of the merchandising set or planogram.

Each year, Progressive Grocer (www.progressivegrocer.com) gives awards to the best category captains. The criteria are as follows:

1. Product innovation
2. Creativity in merchandising, marketing, promotion, and advertising
3. Consumer insights
4. Innovative, dynamic category management tools
5. Demonstrating commitment to meeting the retail consumers' specific needs
6. Effectiveness at differentiating a line or brand within the category
7. Effectiveness at increasing sales for a brand's products in the category
8. Hard evidence of market-specific or account-specific sales results that support the vendor's claims of excellence.

Both the category captains and category advisors have important roles in the criteria used to determine the best planogram or merchandising strategy.

Although the category captain arrangement has become very important to the success of retailers, this arrangement is not without problems. Because vendors have access to their competitors' data, there are opportunities to harm their competitors. Some of the major problems cited in lawsuits regarding the category captain arrangement are (1) the ability to exclude rival vendors from the planogram or greatly increase the cost of competing for the rival, and (2) the category captain can use the role to facilitate collusion among rivals or competing retailers. In regard to exclusion, category captains determine which brands, and the sizes within the brands, are included in the planogram. They may limit the amount of shelf space, merchandising opportunities, and promotional advertising given to the other vendors. In regard to collusion, the category captain has access to proprietary data and information that, if shared with another vendor, could be used to exclude other vendors from successfully competing. However, in the end, the retailer makes the decision to accept, reject, or modify the captain's advice. The retailer's overall strategy makes the decisions when implementing category management.

# Core Features of Category Management

Retailers use category management to support their strategic purchasing decisions through the development and implementation of sourcing strategies. The core features of category management are:

1. **Commitment to institutional change.** In order for category management to be successful, the retailer must commit to the entirety of category management. Retailers often implement only processes that are deemed easy or easily adaptable. They may have the "don't rock the boat" or "if it isn't broken, don't fix it" mentality. For example, it may be easy for a retailer to buy and install new equipment that will provide instantaneous sales to the management team. However, the same retailer may not be willing to replace or reassign the buyer or merchandiser because they have worked together for a long time.

2. **Teamwork.** All members of the category management team—including the buyer for the retailer, the vendors, category captains, and category advisors—must work together to ensure the success of the category. This means everyone shares information and insights about the category. Vendors or trading partners often compromise on the space allocated to their brand so that all brands are adequately displayed within a given amount of space. Partnership is the keyword of category management. Everyone must work together to ensure their category's success.

3. **Decisions based on data analysis.** Category management is a retail strategy that uses data prepared by the retailer, vendors, and outside sources—including purveyors of syndicated data—that compiles the sales of a number of retailers. This data includes unit sales, dollar sales, profit margin, and allocated space. The data must be carefully analyzed to produce the best result for the category and retailer.

4. **Comprehensive tools and techniques to assist in analysis, including software applications.** Category management is a technology-driven strategy. Software applications have been developed by several software companies that allow a very sophisticated analysis of data and assist in preparing a visual depiction of the analysis known as a planogram. In addition to the category management software, category management depends on POS data generated by the retailer, syndicated data, and uses EDI to transfer the data from the individual retail units to the corporate headquarters of the retailers and to the vendors.

5. **Linkage between the business needs and sourcing, including the Internet and business intranet**. The Internet provides individuals and businesses with immediate access to information. The intranet controlled by a business or retailer allows the retailer to limit access to sensitive and/or **proprietary data** to only those individuals they determine need access via the Internet. The intranet has been one of the most important additions to retailing technology. The data is transmitted quickly and accurately among the retailer's trading partners.

6. **A history of success.** Category management has been adopted by many retailers throughout the world. Globalization has changed the grocery industry in most industrialized countries. With mergers and acquisitions, increased competition, and lowered margins, grocery retailers have implemented category management worldwide. Category management has become one of the most frequently implemented strategies

offered through the **Efficient Consumer Response (ECR)** initiative. In Chapter 4, we will discuss the entire concept of Efficient Consumer Response, including category management.

7. **Trust.** Trust is the mainstay of a true partnership. Retailers and their vendors share private information once used as leverage in the negotiation process between retailers and vendors. Now access to data is given to all parties in the trade partnership. However, the access is limited by the role each plays. By sharing data through this trusting relationship, retailers and vendors become vulnerable to each other. This vulnerability cannot be violated or the level of trust is diminished. The success of the category depends on the level of trust between the vendors and retailers. In order for the category management process to be successful, all core features must become part of the retailer's strategy and business process. We will further discuss business strategy and business processes in later chapters.

# Review

Category management is a collaborative process whereby retailers and their customers reap the benefit of a focused approach to retail management. Category management is the collaboration between vendors and retailers to provide optimal service to the customer while providing profit and sales to the retailers and vendors. The Partnering Group defines category management as a retailer/vendor process of managing categories as strategic business units, producing enhanced business results focused on delivering customer value and profit and sales for entire groups of products called categories.

The guiding principles of category management are (1) focus on strategic management of a product group, (2) collaboration between retailers and vendors, and (3) satisfying customers' needs. A category is a distinct, manageable group of products or services that customers perceive as related or as substitutes. Retailers implement category management for many reasons; the major ones are designed to eliminate wasted space, and focus only on the merchandise sought by the customers at a given location, thus increasing profit margins.

Technological innovations that enable category management include the Universal Product Code (UPC), electronic data interchange (EDI), and Quick Response (QR). EDI and QR aim to provide both retailers and suppliers with current and immediate information regarding supplies and inventory.

Using category management, vendors and retailers shifted their focus from the brand to the category. With brand management, the success of the brand was paramount; with category management, the success of the category is paramount. The category management team includes the retail buyer, merchandisers, and vendors. The retailer names a supplier or vendor as the category captain, and another as an advisor. Several criteria are used to determine the success of a category captain; however, several legal issues with the category captain arrangement have arisen, including collusion with, and exclusion of, other vendors.

The core features of category management are (1) commitment to institutional change, (2) teamwork, (3) data analysis, (4) comprehensive tools and techniques, (5) linkage between business needs and sourcing, (6) a history of success, and (7) trust.

# key terms

Brand management   7
Category   5
Category advisor   9
Category captain   8
Category leader   9
Category manager   8
Category management   4
Consultants   9
Efficient Consumer Response (ECR)   11

Electronic data interchange (EDI)   7
Gross margin   7
Loyalty cards   7
Market data   8
Out-of-stock (OOS)   5
Planograms   6
Point of sale (POS)   6
Proprietary data   10
Quick Response (QR)   7

Stockkeeping unit (SKU)   7
Strategic business unit (SBU)   4
Syndicated data   8
Trade partners   5
Universal Product Code (UPC)   7
Validator   9
Vendors   4

# activities

- Search the Web for the term *category management*. Using information gathered, write your own definition of category management.

# discussion questions

1. Explain category management.
2. Define the term *category*.
3. Explain how technology facilitated the implementation of category management.
4. Explain the difference in the perspective of profit and margin generation based on category management and brand management.
5. How does the category management team work together with the buyer?
6. What are the criteria for a successful category captain as determined by Progressive Grocer?
7. What are the core features of category management?

# references, resources, web sites, and recommended readings

- ACNielsen. http://www.acnielsen.com/
- Association for Convenience and Petroleum Retailing. http://www.nacsonline.com/
- Association of Category Management Professionals. http://www.cpgcatnet.org/
- Cannondale Associates Press Release. http://www.cannondaleassoc.com/
- Corstjens, J., and M. Corstjens. 1995. *Store wars: The battle for mindspace and shelfspace*. New York: Wiley.
- Desrochers, D. M., G. T. Gundlach, and A. A. Foer. 2003. Analysis of antitrust challenges to category captain arrangements. *Journal of Public Policy and Marketing*, 22 (2): 201–215.
- Federal Trade Commission. 2000. http://www.ftc.gov/opa/2003/11/slottingallowance.shtm
- Federal Trade Commission. 2004. *Category management: An interview with FTC commissioner, Thomas B. Leary*. http://www.ftc.gov/speeches/leary/050328abainterview.pdf (accessed March 28, 2005)

- Food and Grocery Information. http://www.igd.com/

- Food Marketing Institute. http://www.fmi.org/

- Kahn, B. E., and L. McAlister. 1977. *Grocery revolution: The new focus on the consumer*. Reading, MA: Addison-Wesley.

- Partnering Group. http://www.thepartneringgroup.com/

- Partnering Group. 1995. *Category management report*. Washington, DC: Joint Industry Project on Efficient Consumer Response.

- Progressive Grocer. http://www.progressivegrocer.com/

- Varley, R. 2001. *Retail product management*. 2nd ed. London: Routledge.

- Wileman, A., and M. Jary. 1997. *Retail power plays: From trading to brand leadership*. New York: New York Publishers Press.

- Zenor, M. 1994. The profit benefits of category management. *Journal of Marketing Research*, 31:202–213.

# RETAIL EVOLUTION
## AND STRATEGIES

**LEARNING GOALS**

On completion of this chapter, the student will be able to:

- Realize the importance of understanding the customers' needs in light of a changing retail environment.
- Discuss the role of retail strategy in the choices retailers make to achieve their goals.
- Compare the pricing strategies of everyday low pricing and high–low pricing.
- Contrast the service strategies of the productivity loop and the experiential loop.
- Give examples of the changes and evolution of assortment planning.
- Explain the relationship between technology and retailing.
- Summarize the evolution of space management to category management in the consumer packaged goods industry.

2

# Introduction

In the beginning most retail businesses were family-owned establishments in downtown business districts. The prevailing retail strategy was to be all things to all people, while focused on serving their primary clientele. The next retail evolution was to form chains of stores instead of stand-alone retail stores in order to maximize buying opportunities and minimize costs. As the chains developed, retailers, particularly grocery stores, faced a number of challenges, including an inherent low profit margin, high levels of competition, and an assortment that included many perishable products. As retailers began to expand their territories, they started competing on a number of criteria including price and assortment. Globalization also impacted retailers throughout the world. Retailers responded by improving supply chain management and implementing category management. In order to compete successfully, grocery retailers began to focus on (1) pricing strategy, (2) service strategy, and (3) assortment strategy.

Category management became imperative because of these changes in the retail environment. Two major forces enabled the retail industry to develop category management: (1) innovations in retail technology, and (2) the recognition of the need to meet the needs of the customer through assortment planning. This chapter begins by discussing the primary retailing strategies leading to the development of category management, and the innovations in retail technology that enable the implementation of these strategies and category management. The chapter concludes by discussing the implementation of category management in the consumer packaged goods industry.

# Retail Strategy

Strategy is a long-term plan of action to achieve goals based on a series of decisions. Category management is a corporate strategy used by retailers based on the company mission statement, financial goals, consumer strategies, product strategies, and total system strategies. Corporate strategy is linked to category strategy through the departmental strategies (e.g., grocery, perishable, or general merchandise) that support the overall corporate strategy. The choice of strategies impacts the effectiveness of category management.

# Pricing Strategy

Many retailers choose a retail pricing strategy based either on **everyday low pricing (EDLP)** or **high–low pricing** (Figure 2.1). Retailers, choosing everyday low pricing, seek to price a product for the long term, negotiating with vendors for the lowest possible price for a long period of time. When customers buy the product, they assume the price will remain consistent and generally do not buy excessive quantities of goods. Manufacturers must offer a consistent pricing structure in order for retailers to implement the everyday low pricing strategy. This eliminates the need for customers to "stock up" or buy in large quantities because the price of the product is lower than usual. Retailers using everyday low pricing strategy generally offer (1) a large

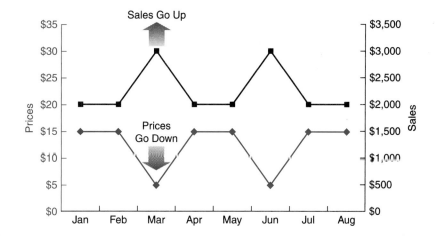

FIGURE 2.1 *High–Low Pricing*

number of products, (2) a smaller selection of brands, and (3) less convenient format. This format appeals to the cost-conscious shopper.

Retailers using high–low pricing typically offer (1) a more convenient format, (2) high-quality service, and (3) a good assortment of products. The high–low retailer competes on service and assortment, not price. They rely on sales and promotions to entice the buyer. Retailers choosing high–low pricing anticipate large fluctuations in the retail and wholesale price. The cycle begins when the manufacturer offers high–low pricing by discounting a given product for a limited period of time to the retailer. The retailer buys in large quantities and warehouses the products until they are needed as stock in stores; this is called **forward buying**. The retailer then offers the customer a discounted price on the goods for a short time, for example, the "weekly special."

Although both strategies have advantages and disadvantages, the high–low strategy may become a burden for the retailer. Customers begin to expect weekly specials where they buy in bulk, causing an increase in demand for shelf space and increased stocking costs to maintain an inventory for that product. In addition, retailers must invest funds for warehouse space. Customers typically "stock up" by purchasing large quantities, then do not purchase again until their supply is depleted. This pricing structure causes large fluctuations in the sales of the promoted products.

Both retailers and their customers participate in forward buying by simply buying excess product during a sale. Retailers are unable to adequately predict the buying patterns of their customers when a cycle of high–low pricing and forward buying is practiced. Manufacturers are then unable to maintain consistency in their level of production. When manufacturers plan to offer lower prices for products to retailers, they must increase production, often meaning higher labor costs. Retailers participating in forward buying must then incur increased storage costs in distribution centers because most retailers have eliminated most of their onsite storage. Retailers do not want to spend money on excess inventory for two reasons: (1) the cost to warehouse the merchandise, and (2) the negative cash flow. When a retailer pays for merchandise before they sell the merchandise, their cash flow is negative. However, there are times when retailers must make a forward buy. Two examples of necessary forward buys are seasonal merchandise and merchandise needed for a special advertisement. The category management team must anticipate the fluctuations in customer demand during promotional periods.

# Service Strategy

In addition to retail pricing strategies, two other strategies are prominent in the grocery industry: (1) the **productivity loop**, and (2) the **experiential loop**. These strategies ultimately impact the level of service offered by the retailer. The productivity loop offers lower prices, but lower levels of service, and limits the assortment. The experiential loop offers higher levels of service, a comprehensive assortment, and higher prices.

The American customer can be characterized as seeking (1) the lowest price available, or (2) an exciting or unique experience with the retailer. Grocers in the United States are designing their stores to meet the needs of these extremes in customer behavior. Some grocers like SuperValu, Food City, Wal-Mart, Bi-Lo, Aldi, and Food Lion seek the value-oriented customers in the majority of their formats. Premium supermarkets like Kroger's Fresh Fare, Whole Foods, and United's Market Street formats serve the customer seeking an exciting or unique experience. The initial costs are higher for experiential retailers; however, over time, the costs generated from the customer experiences are recouped in sales. In contrast, grocery stores seeking the value customer must continually drive down prices and seek new customers to be successful.

The productivity loop, shown in Figure 2.2, is a strategy in which retailers seek to constantly lower costs, thereby lowering prices in the hope that customers will then purchase more goods. When discount retailers began to dominate department stores, the productivity loop became the predominant retail strategy. The challenge of this strategy is maintaining the cycle within the given market constraints. In order to be truly effective with this model, the retailer must constantly attract new customers, maintain current consumers, and continue to lower overall costs. One way to lower costs is to lower the cost of payroll. By lowering payroll, retailers using the productivity loop often offer lowered levels of customer service. The major problem of the productivity loop is the retailer's dependence on the ability to reduce costs. The positive aspects of this strategy peaked in the 1990s when many discounters filed for bankruptcy as costs stabilized at about 17% of sales. This strategy is effective only when a retailer implementing the strategy competes with retailers who are inefficient.

**FIGURE 2.2** *Productivity Loop*

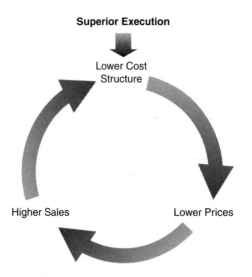

Superior Execution

Lower Cost Structure

Lower Prices

Higher Sales

**FIGURE 2.3** *Experiential Loop*

**Superior Execution**

Increase
Atmospherics

Better Experience

Higher Sales

The experiential retailer offers customers a constant and changing variety of products and experiences by providing a unique environment with a focus on customer service. The retailer focuses on the experience and atmosphere of the store, including product offerings, ambience, and services. Experiential retailers offer a variety of experiences, including aroma therapy massages, coffee shops, concierge services, cooking classes, specialty seminars, food expos, personal shoppers, dieticians, floral designers, cafés, Wi-Fi access, prepared meals, sushi bars, and specialized bakeries for customers seeking a unique shopping experience. These services are all designed to lengthen the time customers spend in a store, and hopefully entice them to buy more merchandise. Whereas the productivity loop seeks to constantly lower costs, the experiential retailer incurs great costs, including specialized labor and elaborate store **atmospherics** to maintain or increase sales to attract more customers and continue to offer new experiences. Atmospherics include all the audio, visual, and scents used by retailers to create an appealing retail space. Figure 2.3 illustrates the experiential loop.

# Assortment Strategy

Family-owned retailers knew which products specific customers preferred and the general quantities they bought. Retail sales history indicates that more products were sold during holidays, birthdays, weddings, and graduations. The retailers anticipated customers' behavior from previous experience and knowledge of the customer. These family businesses specialized in what we now call **customer relationship management (CRM)**. They knew their customers, had a personal relationship with them, and managed to buy the right products to meet their customers' needs. As the chains developed, retailers lost the personal relationship with the customer, and began to seek a new way to plan their merchandise assortment based on customer wants and needs. Retailers began to understand the importance of developing an assortment strategy that both included the desired products while eliminating products that customers were not purchasing. A better assortment eliminates waste in shelf space allocation and improves cash flow.

Retailers began by developing a rudimentary assessment of their sales data, often based on their invoices when they bought merchandise from the manufacturer, wholesaler, or distributor.

As retail chains evolved, retailers began to realize that customers at every store were not the same. Stores in areas where families with young children lived bought different products than areas where older couples lived. For instance, families with young children were more likely to purchase children's clothing, toys, diapers, and baby formula. Although the income levels or ethnicity of both groups may have been similar, their purchasing habits were very different. Simply analyzing their purchase orders or POS data was no longer effective because the purchase indicated only what was purchased, not what was sought and not found, or what products the customer sought elsewhere. Retailers began to classify stores based on the customer demographic and lifestyle characteristics. The assortment was planned to micro market to the customer type. The **assortment** is the number of different items in a merchandise category. Retailers must understand the link between the number of items offered in a category and assortment from the customer's perspective. The **breadth** of an assortment is the number of categories and the **depth** is the number of products in each of the categories.

# Technology and Retailing

The evolution of retailing, including the need to plan multiple assortments, challenged retailers to develop new strategies—including the improvement of supply chain efficiency—to meet the needs of their customers. Many innovations began with retail technology or changes in the retail format. Technology has changed retailing in a number of ways, including supply chain management and space management. **Supply chain management** is the efficient, effective integration of suppliers, manufacturers, warehouses, stores, and transportation intermediaries into a seamless value chain so that merchandise is produced and distributed in the right quantities, to the right locations, and at the right time, to minimize system-wide costs while satisfying the service levels required by customers. The implementation of technology in the management of the supply chain is called **Collaboration, Planning, Forecasting, and Replenishment (CPFR).** CPFR is the integrator that enables all ECR improvement concepts, including category management. A major change in the way retailers think is moving from the traditional marketing channel to supply chain management. The traditional marketing channel begins with the manufacturer; supply chain management begins with the customers purchasing the goods and follows the orders upstream. CPFR has many components, including category management, replenishment planning, logistics and distribution, and store execution. The basics of CPFR are a continuous cycle of four stages: (1) strategy and planning, (2) demand and supply management, (3) execution, and (4) analysis. CPFR is shown in Figure 2.4.

The strategy and planning stage includes category management, a collaborative arrangement between the vendor and retailer. The demand and supply management stage includes forecasting sales and planning to replenish when the sales occur. The execution stage includes ordering and distributing goods. The analysis stage includes store execution and reviewing the performance of all parties of the supply chain. Although the cycle appears to begin with strategy and planning, in actuality there is no beginning or ending. Just as one step ends, the next begins, a continuous cycle like a ring. CPFR has several benefits:

1. CPFR improves the responsiveness to the customer's demand by reducing out-of-stocks and shortening cycle times, thereby putting the right product in the right place at the right time in the right quantities.

Analysis

Strategy &
Planning

Execution

Demand &
Supply Management

FIGURE 2.4  *Collaboration, Planning, Forecasting, and Replenishment (CPFR)*

2. CPRR combines the knowledge of all participants in the supply chain. This knowledge is generated by collecting consumer data, past retail experience of the partners, and research data.

3. Trading partners improve their relationships because of the collaboration through direct communication and regularly exchanging of information.

4. Sales are increased by forecasting potential out-of-stocks and lost sales, and maximizes overall sales for all supply chain partners.

5. Inventory levels may be reduced based on the sales forecast.

6. Overall cost is reduced because manufacturers can predict sales, and thereby plan their production schedules, subsequently reducing capital, handling, and administration costs. (ECR Europe 2001).

Another innovation in retailing that enables assortment planning is space management. The origin of space management was a visual depiction of a planogram. This manual process enables retailers to plan the assortment for each specific store, and prepare a visual depiction or planogram (POG) of the planned merchandise display based on the needs of the specific customer base; see Figure 2.5.

FIGURE 2.5  *Planogram*  (Courtesy of JDA Software Group)

Unfortunately, today's retail technology did not exist and the work was very tedious. This process became known as space management, and the persons working in this role were generally known as **space managers**. Space managers managed the space on a shelf to optimize the space and increase sales. The process was also very slow, but extremely important in the successful execution of the retail process. Space managers used a **magnet board**, with hand-drawn lines to represent shelves and magnets to represent products in a planogram. The space manager placed magnets on the board in the correct order for the store, with the correct number of **facings** beside the correct competing products. A facing is the number of products on a shelf facing the customer. If a mistake was made on any row, the space manager began the row again by rearranging all of the magnets on the row. When finished, the board was photographed and the process began again for another store or type of merchandise. This process was very time consuming, and also had to include time to process the photographic film and mail the planograms to the store. This is how category management or space management began.

In time, engineers began to see the potential for developing software products to increase the efficiency of the process. Instead of using a magnet board, they developed software programs that allow space managers to prepare a planogram on a computer screen. The benefits are numerous. With a software program, when a mistake is made or the planogram needs to be adjusted, the products are moved visually to another location or deleted from the merchandising set. The time necessary to complete a planogram is significantly reduced. In addition, the space manager develops a library of planograms he or she can use in the future by making small changes, or use an older planogram as a template to develop new ones for similar stores. Furthermore, electronic files can be easily shared via email, Internet, or intranet between retailers and vendors.

As space management programs evolved, the process became more data intensive. Data are analyzed in the software program, including point of sale (POS) data and syndicated data, both of which offer insight into customer behavior. Through an analysis of customer behavior, retailers have determined the paths the majority of customers walk on a given aisle. Many major retailers use cameras to watch customers' shopping behavior, including their traffic patterns, time spent on an aisle, and the shelf they are mostly likely to reach for or view. When a retailer knows the path the majority of customers walk (traffic pattern), they may then plan a strategy to determine which products they want the customer to see first when entering an aisle. They also know the shelf from which customers most frequently purchase. Software programs allow the retailer to indicate the direction in which the customer walks when preparing the planograms; see Figure 2.5. In addition, retailers prepare the planograms based on the location of the primary entrance to the store, for instance, whether the store has a left or right entrance. The role of space manager has evolved into a role in category management, where an entire category of products is managed based on POS and syndicated data and customer behavior research. There are additional key changes for retailers:

1. Individual categories are operated as separate businesses within a store.
2. The responsibility for advertising, promotions, pricing, and merchandising is consolidated under one category manager.
3. Financial performance is tracked at the category level, not the department level.
4. Key suppliers are treated as strategic business partners and involved in the planning process.

# Implementation of Category Management in Consumer Packaged Goods

The mainstay of many retailers is consumer packaged goods. These retailers include, but are not limited to, grocery stores, auto supply stores, drug stores, pet stores, convenience stores, home improvement stores, dollar stores, and craft stores. Any retail type using gondolas to stock and sell products can implement category management. A gondola is a metal fixture with shelves, usually about 4 feet wide, 6 feet high, and 2 feet deep. In the United States, a product typically sold in recognizable packaging that sells on a consistent basis is called a **consumer packaged good (CPG)**; in Europe, they are often called **fast moving consumer goods (FMCG)**. A CPG is a product in a standard package such as a box, jar, can, or bottle containing products normally sold on a gondola. Examples are spaghetti sauce, soap, toothpaste, canned soup, detergent, dog food, soft drinks, over-the-counter medications, cosmetics, milk products, automotive oil, anti-freeze, and paint.

For a retailer to successfully implement category management, they must implement retail technology throughout the process. The category manager focuses on inventory, space, and consumer traffic in order to increase sales and profitability. A retailer marking each item with a pricing gun and/or hand keying the price of the good at the checkout probably has not implemented category management or most common retail technologies. Even the use of scanners by retailers does not ensure that the retailer has implemented category management. The most effective and efficient applications of category management are in consumer packaged goods; however, retailers are implementing retail technology and category management in **softlines** (clothing, footwear, jewelry, linens, and towels) effectively. The implementation of category management necessitated the need to capture data on consumer buying behavior and enhanced logistics.

Different strategies that retailers use impact the overall implementation of category management. The impact of retail strategy can easily be seen in the strategies and tactics of category management: advertising, promotions, pricing, assortment planning, merchandising, and shelf space allocation. Ensuing chapters discuss the specific details of the category management business process in more detail.

# Review

In the beginning most retail businesses were family businesses in downtown business districts, then chains of stores developed. As retailing began to evolve, retailers developed mission statements and began to make decisions based on strategies related to pricing, customer service, and assortment planning. The choices impacted the implementation of category management. The two prevalent pricing structures in grocery retailing are everyday low pricing and high–low pricing, and were based on the productivity loop and experiential loop.

Technology changed retailing in a number of ways, including supply chain management and space management. Supply chain management is the efficient, effective integration of suppliers, manufacturers, warehouses, stores, and transportation intermediaries into a seamless value chain with the ultimate goal of lowering costs. Space management is the strategy that aims to optimize space to increase sales. This strategy ultimately evolved into category management with the advent of technological applications. Categories of products were managed based on data from POS systems, syndicated data, and customer behavior research. Categories were operated as if separate business units within a store. Category managers were responsible for advertising, promotions, pricing, and merchandising of the category. Financial performance was tracked at the category level, rather than the department level. Key suppliers became strategic business partners and became involved in the planning process.

# key terms

| | | |
|---|---|---|
| Assortment   20 | Customer relationship | Forward buying   17 |
| Atmospherics   19 | management (CRM)   19 | High–low pricing   16 |
| Breadth   20 | Depth   20 | Magnet board   22 |
| Collaboration, Planning, | Everyday low pricing (EDLP)   16 | Productivity loop   18 |
| Forecasting, and Replenishment | Experiential loop   18 | Softlines   23 |
| (CPFR)   20 | Facings   22 | Supply chain management   20 |
| Consumer packaged goods   23 | Fast moving consumer goods (FMCG)   23 | |

# activities

- Research two competing grocery stores in your area. Based on your research and observations, describe and comment on the effectiveness of the retail strategy that these retailers use. Choose one using high–low pricing and one using everyday low prices.

- Contrast two apparel retailers using the experiential loop and productivity loop to attract customers. Give examples of the services they provide, and the price point of each. Explain which retailer you find more interesting as a customer, and as a retail professional.

# discussion questions

1. When family businesses began to evolve into chains, what were the major challenges they faced?
2. Differentiate the everyday low pricing and high–low pricing strategies.
3. Explain the concept of forward buying.
4. Contrast the productivity loop and the experiential loop.
5. Define customer relationship management.
6. How did assortment planning evolve?
7. Define supply chain management.
8. Define and explain CPFR.
9. How did space management evolve from a manual task to category management?

# references, resources, web sites, and recommended readings

- Arkader, R. and C. F. Ferreira. 2004. Category management initiatives from the retailer perspective: A Study in the Brazilian grocery retail industry. *Journal of Purchasing and Supply Management* 10:41–51.

- ECR Europe. 2001. *A Guide to CPFR Implementation.* Spain: ECR Europe and Accentura.

- Harris, J. K. and M. McPartland. 1993. Category Management Defined: What it is and why it works. *Progressive Grocer,* 72 (9): 5–8.

- Singh, J. and R. Blattberg. 2001. *New generation category management.* Category Management, Inc. London: Datamonitor PLC.

- Steidtmann, C. 2002. *Reinventing retail: The challenge of demand chain innovation.* New York: Deloitte Research.

- The Wharton School of the University of Pennsylvania. 2000. *How store location and pricing structure affect shopping behavior.* Pennsylvania: Knowledge@ Wharton. http://knowledge.wharton.upenn.edu/articlepdf/203.pdf (accessed September 19, 2007).

# MEASUREMENTS
## AND PRODUCTIVITY

**LEARNING GOALS**

On completion of this chapter, the student will be able to:

- Explain the concept of markup and markdowns.
- Understand and compute maintained markups.
- Define measures of assets.
- Define measures of performance.
- Understand Activity Based Costing (ABC).
- Understand the application of ABC to category management.

# Introduction

All business people must determine how they will measure success. Success may be the number of visitors to a theme park, the customer service ratings by customers, the number of clients, or numeric measures of productivity focused on retail sales and gross margin. Success can be determined by many different means depending on the type of business; however, retailers most often judge success by numeric measures of productivity focused on retail sales and gross margin. Historically, sales, profit, and markup have been used. **Gross sales** are the total sales made within a given period of time. **Net sales** are the total sales minus any deductions in sales such as customer returns. Both are important in determining the success of a retail store or chain. However, they are only a snapshot of the success. In order to truly measure the success of a retailer, we must also determine the cost to the retailer when generating gross sales or net sales. Cost is the amount that the retailer pays for a product, including the direct cost of the product itself and indirect costs such as transportation and other expenses associated with the preparation and selling of that particular product. In this chapter we review many familiar concepts, and use them to determine more complex measures of productivity.

# Markup

**Markup** or **mark-on** is the difference between the cost of a product and the retail price. Retail price − cost = markup. The **markup percentage** is calculated by taking the amount of markup and dividing it by the retail price. For example, if the retailer determines a markup of $2 for a product that sells for $10, the markup percentage would be 20%. **Initial markup** is the markup placed on the product or stockkeeping unit (SKU). For instance, assuming a retailer purchases Product X for $18 per unit, the retailer sets the price at $36; therefore, the initial markup is $18, or a markup percentage of 50%. Occasionally a retailer's first markup is lower than the eventual markup; the retailer then changes the retail price and increases the markup. When the retailer raises the initial retail price by increasing the markup, this is the **additional markup**. Using the same example for Product X, the retailer raises the markup and retail price by $2. The new retail price for Product X now is $38. The additional markup percentage is 2/38, or 5.3%. However, many retailers change the retail price during sales, changing the markup. The aggregate of the markup on a single SKU is called a **cumulative markup**. For instance, 10 units of Product X are sold at the initial retail price of $36 with a markup of $18, and another 10 units of Product X are sold at the secondary retail price of $38 for a markup of $20. The cumulative markup is determined by calculating the total markup achieved and then dividing by the total sales of the number of units sold, as shown in Figure 3.1.

$$\text{Cumulative Markup Percentage} = (\$18 \times 10) + (\$20 \times 10)/(\$36 \times 10) + (\$38 \times 10)$$
$$= (\$180 + \$200)/(360 + 380)$$
$$= 52.7\%$$

**FIGURE 3.1** *Cumulative Markup Percentage*

| Original Retail Price | $100.00 |
|---|---|
| Less Markdown (25%) | $25.00 |
| New Retail Price | $75.00 |
| Less Additional Markdown (10%) | $7.50 |
| New Retail Price after Additional Markdown | $67.50 |

**FIGURE 3.2** *Calculation of Additional Markdown*

# Markdowns

A **markdown** is lowering the retail price on a stockkeeping unit or SKU. Retailers use markdowns for several reasons. A markdown is typically used to compete with other retailers and to lower inventory levels. Customers expect markdowns at the end of a season or when a newer product within a category is introduced. At the end of a season retailers often offer progressive markdowns—first a 15% markdown, then 25%, 50%, and finally even a higher markdown. Retailers also mark down merchandise when their competitors offer the same SKU at a lower price. The markdown percentage is determined by dividing the markdown dollar by the original retail dollar. For example, a markdown of $25 on a SKU with an original retail price of $100 is 25%. When a series of markdowns occurs, the markdown percent is determined by dividing the dollar markdown by the new retail price. For instance, the new retail price on the SKU above is $75; if a new markdown percentage is 10%, the new markdown is $7.50. The calculations are shown in Figure 3.2. The markdown rate for a period of time is determined by adding the total markdown dollars for the period divided by the net sales for the period.

There are several types of markdowns, including markdowns for damaged goods, employee discounts, promotional markdowns (temporary markdowns), or clearance markdowns. Damaged goods may include dents or missing parts such as buttons. These damaged goods or products are usually sold "as is," meaning there are usually restrictions on exchanges or returns. Most retailers offer discounts to their employees, usually in a standard percentage form for all goods and services purchased by the employees. A promotional discount is a temporary discount taken during a promotional period when the SKU is advertised at a lower price. Clearance markdowns are permanent markdowns taken (1) at the end of a season, (2) when goods are discontinued, (3) when an assortment is broken, or (4) the merchandise is a slow seller. A broken assortment is when all of the items within an assortment are no longer available, such as the assortment has only blue tops and red skirts. Merchandise can become a slow seller due to any number of reasons, including (1) atypical weather, (2) an unappealing assortment purchased by a buyer, (3) the merchandise is displayed on fixtures in a low traffic area or displayed poorly, or (4) the merchandise arrived too late to compete with other brands or retailers with similar merchandise.

# Maintained Markup

**Maintained markup** is the difference between the cost of the merchandise and the actual selling price (Figure 3.3).

> Maintained Markup = Initial Markup + Additional Markup − Markdowns

**FIGURE 3.3** *Maintained Markup*

Using the earlier example of Product X, the initial markup of $18 is later increased with an additional markup of $2. Assuming that later the retailer marks down Product X by $4, the maintained markup for Product X is = $18 + $2 − $4 = $16.

**Gross margin** is the difference between the total cost of a good and the total retail sales. Gross margin = maintained markup − transportation costs − workroom costs + cash discounts. Transportation costs are the costs associated with the transport of products, including shipping expenses. Workroom costs are the costs associated with preparing goods for retail sale, such as alterations of men's slacks or women's bridal dresses. A cash discount is offered when retailers pay for the merchandise before or on a specific date. For instance, a typical cash discount is 2/10, net 30—by paying the invoice within 10 days of the invoice, the retailer receives a 2% discount; otherwise, the entire invoice is due in 30 days.

As retailing evolved, most retailers determined their productivity based on gross margin. However, mass merchandisers changed the importance of the equation. Mass merchandisers, or discount stores, typically chose the productivity loop when determining the strategy they would use to operate their businesses. The productivity loop states that the retailer should decrease the markup or negotiate for a lower cost (from the suppliers) to increase overall sales.

Using the traditional gross margin formula, the true success of the retailer with a low margin and high sales is not adequately assessed. When retailers are judged by retail analysts at the end of a quarter or by the retailer's annual report, these retailers' success was minimized. Analysts and retailers began to realize that the formula was inadequate and developed the **Gross Margin Return on Inventory Investment (GMROII)** assessment tool; see Figure 3.4. GMROII allows retailers to compare the performance of departments, vendors, stores, and customer groups, whereas assessing only gross margin did not allow for a true comparison. Margin is the difference between the retail price and the cost. Products with a high margin, such as jewelry, could not be compared to products with a low margin. GMROII accounts for both margin and turn. For instance, would you rather sell Product A with a retail price of $20 and a $10 margin (50%) and a stock turn of 4, or sell Product B with a retail price of $4 and $1 margin (25%) and a stock turn of 200?

Using the example of Products A and B above, the GMROII calculations are:

Product A = $40/$10 = 4.00      or      $(0.50 \times 4)/(1 − 0.50) = 4.00$
Product B = $200/$3 = 66.67     or      $(0.25 \times 200)/(1 − 0.25) = 66.67$

> GMROII = Gross Margin $/Average Inventory Cost
> Or
> GMROII = (Gross Margin % × Stock Turns)/1 − Gross Margin %

**FIGURE 3.4** *Gross Market Return on Inventory Investment (GMROII) Formula*

TABLE 3.1

| | Retail | | | Stock | Overall |
| Product | Price | Margin | Margin % | Turn | Profit |
| --- | --- | --- | --- | --- | --- |
| A | $20 | $10 | 50% | 4 | $40 |
| B | $4 | $1 | 25% | 200 | $200 |

As shown in Table 3.1, with Product A you make a profit of $40 and with Product B you make a profit of $200. If you simply compared the margin, you could not accurately assess the profitability of each; you must look at the effect of the stock turn to adequately determine the gross margin of the two products.

# Measures of Assets

In category management we measure productivity in a number of ways to determine how well space is used to sell the number of units available and the number of dollars generated. By measuring performance and assets we can determine a measure of productivity for a product or category of merchandise.

There are three measures of assets: (1) space, (2) capacity, and (3) inventory dollars. An important measure for retailers is in determining how space is used to generate sales. Space is measured in three ways: (1) **square feet**, (2) **linear feet**, and (3) **cubic feet**. A typical measure is Sales per Square Foot when reporting retail sales; fashion retailers most often report sales by square foot. For instance, a retailer may report sales as $600 per square foot. In other words, over the period of a year a store with 1,500 square feet (30 feet wide and 50 feet deep) has sales of $300,000 (600 × 1,500). A typical 12″ × 12″ floor tile is 1 square foot. A square foot is a two-dimensional measurement of space, length × width. Linear feet refers to the number of feet in a straight line of a shelf, typically used for a measurement of shelf space productivity. For instance, a shelf that is 30 feet long occupies a space of 30 linear feet. The third method is cubic feet. A cubic foot is three dimensional, which includes length, depth, and height. For instance, the length of a shelf (30′) × depth (2′) × height of space above shelf (2′) = 120 cubic feet.

The second factor in determining asset productivity is **inventory units or capacity**. Inventory units or capacity are the number of products that fit on a shelf—across the front of the shelf, to the back of shelf, and the number of products stacked on each other. If you think about boxes of puzzles on a shelf, you can picture capacity. The third measure of assets is inventory dollars (capacity × unit cost). This is how much money is used to fill a shelf. Think about IPods; how much money does the retailer have to invest in IPods to fill a shelf?

# Measures of Performance

The first measure of performance is **Movement per Square Foot**, or movement/space. How many times does the merchandise turn? For instance, if the puzzles have a stock turn of 12 and use 4 linear feet, the movement per linear foot is 12/4 = 3 per linear foot. This measures

| Movement Per Square Foot = Stock Turn/Square Foot |
| --- |

**FIGURE 3.5** *Movement Per Square Foot Formula*

| Sales Per Square Foot = Sales/Square Foot |
| --- |

**FIGURE 3.6** *Sales Per Square Foot Formula*

| Profit Per Square Foot = Total Profit/Total Square Foot |
| --- |

**FIGURE 3.7** *Profit Per Square Foot Formula*

the movement generated per foot of space allocated; in other words, it measures the productivity of the space in generating customer traffic.

Another measure of performance is **Sales per Square Foot**, or sales/space. This calculation shows how productive the space is in generating sales. For example, if a retailer has IPod sales of $600 that are displayed on 4 linear feet, the sales are 600/4 = $150 per linear foot. This is a measure of how many dollars are generated per foot of space allocated.

Although the Sales per Square Foot is valuable information for a retailer, combining this information with the **Profit per Square Foot** yields a more meaningful result. The Profit per Square Foot shows the productivity of space in generating profit, and is calculated by dividing the total profit by the total square feet. For instance, if the puzzles generate $50 total profit, the Profit per Square Foot is $50/4 = $12.50 per foot. If the IPods generate $300 total profit, the Profit per Square Foot is $300/4 = $75 per foot. The IPods generate higher profit and sales than puzzles.

**Shelf turns** is the measure of stocking efficiency related to the use of shelf space. It measures the number of times the merchandise on a shelf turns over. To calculate shelf turns, you use a movement/capacity formula. This is a measure of sell through, of how many times you sell all of the units on a shelf during a year. For instance, if there are 20 boxes of puzzles (capacity) on a shelf and the annual movement is 12, the shelf turns would be 12/20 = 0.60, or 60%. A shelf turns ratio of less than 1.00 means that the product did not completely sell through during the year (or operating period). The ratio of 0.60 reveals that out of the 20 puzzles on the shelf, only 60%, or 12 puzzles, were sold in a year.

**Days of Supply** is a measure of inventory efficiency, and is especially useful to retailers when used to coordinate with delivery and stocking schedules. For example, if a grocer has enough space for only 20 cartons of milk (capacity) in the cooler section and 40 cartons are sold each day (movement), the Days of Supply would be 20/40 = 0.50, or half a day. This grocer would have to restock the milk each day to keep up with the demand.

| Shelf Turns = Movement/Capacity |
|---|

**FIGURE 3.8** *Shelf Turns Formula*

| Days of Supply = Capacity/Daily Movement |
|---|

**FIGURE 3.9** *Days of Supply Formula*

# Activity Based Costing

**Activity Based Costing**, commonly referred to as ABC, is organizing costs of key activities to a related product or products. To better understand the purpose of ABC, one has to first understand the concept of direct and indirect costs. Direct costs are costs that can be easily identified with a product, such as the purchase price of merchandise. Indirect costs are costs that are not directly associated with a product or products. Examples of indirect costs are expenses, such as sales, operating, and administrative. Most businesses assign indirect costs to a product, or category of products, by applying a predetermined percentage. For example, the total operating expense of $10,000 may be distributed to five different products under a category, with each absorbing 20% or $2,000. The benefit of this method is that it is very simple to calculate. However, this method assumes that the operating effort required of the five products is equal. Generally, under this traditional method, a product that is difficult or requires more effort seems to have lower operating expenses. Table 3.2 illustrates the traditional distribution of indirect costs. Assume that a business sells a total of 10,000 units in five different products, and incurs a total operating expense of $40,000. Under the traditional method, the operating expense would be determined by taking the $40,000 and dividing it by 10,000 units, which equals $4.00 of operating expense per unit, as shown in Table 3.2.

| TABLE 3.2 | | | | | |
|---|---|---|---|---|---|
| **Calculate Unit Operating Expense Using Traditional Accounting** | | | | | |
| **TOTAL OPERATING EXEPNSES = $40,000** | | | | | |
| **Product** | **Unit Retail Price** | **Units Sold** | **Unit Operating Expense** | **Unit Profit Margin** | **Margin %** |
| A | $ 8.00 | 3,000 | $4.00 | $ 4.00 | 50% |
| B | $10.00 | 2,500 | $4.00 | $ 6.00 | 60% |
| C | $12.00 | 2,000 | $4.00 | $ 8.00 | 67% |
| D | $15.00 | 1,500 | $4.00 | $11.00 | 73% |
| E | $18.00 | 1,000 | $4.00 | $14.00 | 78% |
| | Total | 10,000 | | | |

**TABLE 3.3**

### Calculate Unit Operating Expense Using Activity Based Costing (ABC)

| Product | Unit Retail Price | Units Sold | Operating Steps per Unit | Total Operating Steps | Driver Rate | Unit Operating Expense | Unit Profit Margin | Margin % |
|---|---|---|---|---|---|---|---|---|
| A | $ 8.00 | 3,000 | 1 | 3,000 | $1.60 | $1.60 | $ 6.40 | 80% |
| B | $10.00 | 2,500 | 2 | 5,000 | $1.60 | $3.20 | $ 6.80 | 68% |
| C | $12.00 | 2,000 | 3 | 6,000 | $1.60 | $4.80 | $ 7.20 | 60% |
| D | $15.00 | 1,500 | 4 | 6,000 | $1.60 | $6.40 | $ 8.60 | 57% |
| E | $18.00 | 1,000 | 5 | 5,000 | $1.60 | $8.00 | $10.00 | 56% |
| | Total | 10,000 | | 25,000 | | | | |

Because the unit operating expense is the same for all the products, Product E, which has a higher retail price, will show a higher unit profit margin and margin percentage (before direct costs). In this case, Product A shows only a 50% profit margin versus Product E with a 78% profit margin. Common sense dictates that the product with a higher retail price should be associated with higher operating expenses. In this case, the traditional method artificially increases the profit margin of the product with a higher selling price.

Using the same example as above, let's assume with further analysis that the business is able to determine the true activities that go into selling each of the five products. The operating steps required for each product is shown in Table 3.3. Multiplying the steps required for each product with the total number of units sold reveals the total operating steps for each product. For example, the total operating steps required for Product A is 3,000 steps (1 × 3000) versus 5,000 steps (5 × 1000). Once all the operating steps are calculated for each product, the overall steps for all the products are totaled; in this case, there are 25,000 total steps. Next, we divide the $40,000 operating expense by the total steps to get the driver rate, or rate per step. We take the driver rate of $1.60 ($40,000/25,000), then multiply it by the operating steps per unit to find the unit operating expense.

You can clearly see the difference in unit operating expense using the ABC method versus the traditional method (Table 3.4). For example, Product A now has a unit operating expense

**TABLE 3.4**

### Compare traditional accounting and Activity Based Costing (ABC)

| Product | Unit Retail Price | Units Sold | TRADITIONAL ACCOUNTING Unit Operating Expense | Unit Profit Margin | Margin % | ABC Unit Operating Expense | Unit Profit Margin | Margin % |
|---|---|---|---|---|---|---|---|---|
| A | $ 8.00 | 3,000 | $4.00 | $ 4.00 | 50% | $1.60 | $ 6.40 | 80% |
| B | $10.00 | 2,500 | $4.00 | $ 6.00 | 60% | $3.20 | $ 6.80 | 68% |
| C | $12.00 | 2,000 | $4.00 | $ 8.00 | 67% | $4.80 | $ 7.20 | 60% |
| D | $15.00 | 1,500 | $4.00 | $11.00 | 73% | $6.40 | $ 8.60 | 57% |
| E | $18.00 | 1,000 | $4.00 | $14.00 | 78% | $8.00 | $10.00 | 56% |

of $1.60, a decrease of $3.20 per unit. Product E shows an increase of $4.00 per unit in operating expense.

Keep in mind the overall operating expense of $40,000; the total sales, and the total profit, did not change. ABC redistributes the operating expenses to each product according to only their true activities to accurately show the expenses incurred by each product.

# Application to Category Management

We now know the formulas and definitions for measures of productivity, but now need to apply them to a real life scenario. A retailer has been operating business as usual, filling gondolas and refrigerated cases with merchandise ordered in the past. When the shelf becomes empty, the retailer restocks the merchandise. The merchandise assortment is determined by vendors' recommendations and the retailer's past experience. The retailer notices a slow decline in gross sales, net sales, and gross margin. The retailer brings in a consultant to help determine where the retailer needs to make improvements. The first step is to review all of the quantitative data, including sales, markups, markdowns, costs, and gross margins. These are the typical measures of retail success. However, the category management consultant begins a more in-depth analysis. Category management wants to reduce the Days of Supply, increase the profit dollars, reduce out-of stocks, and ultimately make the merchandising more attractive.

The first step in the analysis is to review the POS data, including determining the sales per SKU, the number of facings per SKU, and the cost per SKU. There are three kinds of measures when evaluating a planogram: performance, assets, and productivity. Performance measures include movement, sales, gross profit, space, inventory units or capacity, and inventory dollars (capacity × unit cost).

# Review

Retailers often measure success by focusing on sales and gross margin. To understand sales and gross margin, one must also understand the concept of **markup** or **mark-on**. **Markup** is the difference between the cost of a product and the retail price. The **markup percentage** is calculated by taking the amount of markup and dividing it by the retail price. A retailer may increase the markup on a particular product over time with **additional markup**. The aggregate of the markup on a single SKU is called a **cumulative markup**.

**Retailers also use markdown**, lowering the retail price on a SKU, to increase sales, lower inventory levels, and many other reasons. Most often, customers associate markdown with end-of-season merchandise. Combining the initial markup with the additional markups and subtracting the total markdowns gives you the **maintained markup**, which is the difference between the cost of the merchandise and the actual selling price.

Retailers also use **Gross Margin Return on Inventory Investment (GMROII)** to assess performance. GMROII accounts for both margin and turn.

In category management productivity is measured in a number of ways, including the measure of assets. There are three measures of assets: (1) space, (2) capacity, and (3) inventory dollars. As a measure of performance, space productivity is often reported as sales per **square feet**, **linear feet**, or **cubic feet**.

Capacity or inventory units are the number of products that fit on a shelf across the front of the shelf, to the back of the shelf, and the number of products stacked on each other.

# key terms

# activities

- Read the Harvard Business School Working Papers: Time-Driven Activity-Based Costing (http://hbswk.hbs.edu/item/5436.html) and Rethinking Activity-Based Costing (http://hbswk.hbs.edu/item/4587.html)

- Think about a recent shopping experience. List all of the steps in the shopping experience, beginning with you leaving your home. Assign a cost to each activity, including driving based on your hourly wage or the minimum wage.

# discussion questions

1. How many times does the merchandise turn if it has a stock turn of 24 and uses 6 inches of space?

2. How productive is space in generating sales when sales of printers are $420 and are displayed on 2 feet of space?

3. How productive is space in generating profit when laptops generate $150 profit in 6 linear feet?

4. What is the shelf turn of a shelf holding 24 toys with a stock turn of 8?

5. What is the Days of Supply for juice on a shelf holding 40 units at a given time and daily movement of 4?

# references, resources, web sites and recommended readings

- Easterling, C. R., E. L. Flottman, M. H. Jernigan, and B. E. S. Wuest. 2007. *Merchandising math for retailing*. 4th ed. Upper Saddle River, NJ: Prentice Hall.

- Petersen, J. A., L. McAlister, D. J. Reibstein, R. S. Winer, V. Kumar, G. Atkinson. 2009. Choosing the right metrics to maximize profitability and shareholder value. *Journal of Retailing* 85(1): 95–111.

# RETAIL VALUE
# CHAIN MANAGEMENT

**LEARNING GOALS**

On completion of this chapter, the student will be able to:

- Define value chain management, and apply the concept to retailing.
- Explain the impact of Quick Response and Total Quality Management on Efficient Consumer Response (ECR).
- List the key attributes of ECR.
- List the five guiding principles of ECR.
- Discuss the origin of ECR in relationship to traditional retailing.
- Explain the purpose of efficient assortment.
- List the technological changes in retailing that improved the process of replenishment.
- Discuss the challenges in developing efficient promotions.
- Discuss the benefits of testing new products prior to introduction.
- List the benefits of ECR.

4

# Introduction

Value chain management is a term coined by Michael Porter in *Competitive Advantage: Creating and Sustaining Superior Performance* (1985). A **value chain** is a flow of processes in which a product gains value. This chapter applies the value chain concept to retailing, thus the retail value chain. Five factors lead to the development of the retail value chain:

1. Competitive and structural changes in the retail industry
2. Intensified price competition
3. Growing number of private label products
4. Power of global retail giants over suppliers
5. Competition between players and extended value chains

The management and improvement of the retail value chain has been an evolutionary processes. Three major movements within the retail industry have enabled the development of the retail value chain:

1. Quick Response (QR)
2. Efficient Consumer Response (ECR) models of 1992 and 1996
3. Collaboration, Planning, Forecasting, and Replenishment (CPFR)

# Quick Response

As discussed in Chapter 1, the Quick Response (QR) Initiative was a strategy developed by the apparel industry in the 1980s when the industry felt the challenge of imports. QR offered manufacturers a competitive advantage through a combination of strategies designed to reduce inventory levels, improve merchandise quality, increase worker productivity, increase stock turnover, and reduce merchandise markdowns and inventory costs (Kurt Salmon Associates 1997). An additional key factor was the use of technology to review current practices and develop a collaborative environment between retailers and suppliers. Each of these concepts became a foundation for the development of the ECR movement in the retail industry, particularly in the grocery sector.

# Development of Efficient Consumer Response

The ECR movement was developed as a retail management strategy in the 1990s to improve the supply chain in food retailing. The purpose was for retailers, wholesalers, and suppliers to create and sustain competitive advantage by making the supply chain more competitive and to bring greater value to the grocery consumer. ECR was the first time retailers and suppliers worked together to develop a concrete framework for working together to improve operating practices for both parties. ECR drew from best practices in the grocery industry as well as other industry strategies, such as QR in the general merchandise industry and **Total Quality Management (TQM)** in the manufacturing industry. TQM was a movement in the 1950s to improve quality by involving all parties involved in the production of a product. Another related outcome of these strategies is the Collaboration, Planning, Forecasting, and Replenishment Model. These processes are all part of the strategic management used by retailers to improve the retail value chain. Strategic management is the analysis, decisions, and actions an organization undertakes to create and sustain a competitive advantage. Four key attributes are important in the implementation of ECR related to the implementation of strategic management:

1. Direct the organization toward overall goals and objectives.
2. Include all stakeholders in decision making.
3. Incorporate both short-term and long-term perspectives.
4. Recognize trade-offs between efficiency and effectiveness.

The major obstacle in implementing ECR is organizational. The advocacy of the Chief Operating Officer (CEO) is crucial. The CEO is responsible for directing the organization in regard to the overall goals and objectives. They are also responsible for including all stakeholders in the decision-making process while developing both short-term and long-term perspectives. With any organizational change, there are tradeoffs. Implementing ECR requires new measurement systems. In addition to traditional measures of efficiency and effectiveness, new measures are also necessary, including the improved costing system of Activity Based Costing discussed in Chapter 3.

Manufacturers, wholesalers, and retailers work together as business allies to reduce overall costs, inventories, and physical assets while providing improved consumer choice. Efficient consumer response has five guiding principles:

1. Focus on providing better value to the consumer: better product, better quality, better assortment, better in-stock service, and better convenience with less cost throughout the total chain.
2. ECR must be driven by committed business leaders who are willing to change the once-adversarial relationships between retailers and vendors in order to achieve profitability.
3. Accurate and timely information is necessary for effective marketing, production, and logistic decisions. The information must flow between trading partners using electronic data interchange (EDI) technology.
4. Product flow focuses on providing the right product at the right time to the right consumer.
5. Performance is measured by the effectiveness of the total system, including reduced costs, lower inventory levels, increased revenue, and profit. ECR promotes the equitable sharing of those rewards between partners.

Very simply, ECR was designed to combine the two concepts from the mom-and-pop stores of (1) meeting the needs of the consumer, and (2) fully using retailers' limited shelf space to maintain expected profitability levels. The efficient part of the definition was defined as having the right product in the right place at the right time in the right quantities, a basic marketing principle. ECR has saved the grocery industry billions of dollars by reducing supply chain inventory by 41% and reducing the average days of supply from 104 to 61 days (Kurt Salmon Associates 1993).

ECR began because grocery stores and their trading partners were operating on a very small profit margin, or markup. Margin or markup is the difference between retail price and cost. Both began to realize that there had to be a better, more efficient way to conduct business. Both grocers and their trading partnersor suppliers (vendors, distributors, and brokers) were interested in the success of the grocery industry. Once adversaries; grocers, vendors, distributors, and brokers became true partners in the process by sharing information and setting mutual goals (Kurt Salmon Associates 1993).

During the late 1980s and early 1990s, a recession—combined with the growth of private label products, and a proliferation of new retail formats, such as the warehouse club and supercenter—gave the grocery industry incentive to change the way they had conducted business. This change was led by a group of industry leaders who formed the Efficient Consumer Response Working Group in the mid-1990s. They commissioned a major study to determine how the grocery industry could save tens of billions of dollars. This initiative became the most ambitious project in grocery retailing since the implementation of the UPC code. This group, known as the Joint Industry Project, began to analyze each link in the supply system and identify methods of cutting costs and improving efficiency, and finally to disseminate the information through a series of reports (Kurt Salmon Associates 1993).

# Benefits and Attributes of ECR

ECR provides both tangible and intangible benefits. The tangible benefits of increasing sales and profit to both the suppliers and retailers are easy to recognize and is the core objective of ECR. The intangible benefits from ECR are just as important. Table 4.1 shows how customers, retailers, and suppliers receive the intangible benefits from ECR. These benefits enable customers to have an enhanced retail experience while retailers and suppliers become more successful in both business relationships and branding.

ECR focuses on shortening time and eliminating costs in the supply chain by using the four initiatives of (1) efficient assortments, (2) efficient replenishment, (3) efficient promotions, and (4) efficient product introductions. These initiatives lower the overall costs of business and improve efficiency by decreasing paperwork and relying instead on technology. Each of these initiatives ultimately impact customers' shopping experiences by:

1. Providing an easy-to-shop assortment based on customer wants.
2. Maintaining high in-stock levels of the required assortment.
3. Communicating product benefits and value through advertising and price incentives.
4. Developing and introducing products to meet consumer needs.

The successful implementation of ECR results in better products, quality, assortments, in-stock service, convenience, and value. Figure 4.1 shows the impact of ECR on consumer satisfaction (Kurt Salmon Associates 1993).

Although proponents of ECR have found the process to be beneficial, the adoption of ECR rarely delivers immediate financial benefits. According to some studies, implementing ECR can result in a 5.7% reduction in consumer prices, 4.8% reduction in operating costs, and 0.9% reduction in inventory levels. These numbers will vary across countries, retailers, distribution

## TABLE 4.1

| Intangible Benefits of ECR | | |
|---|---|---|
| **Customers** | **Retailers** | **Suppliers** |
| Increased choice and shopping convenience | Increased consumer loyalty | Reduced out-of-stock items |
| Reduced out-of-stock items | Better informed customer | Enhanced brand integrity |
| Fresher products available for purchase | Improved relationships with suppliers | Improved retailer relationships |

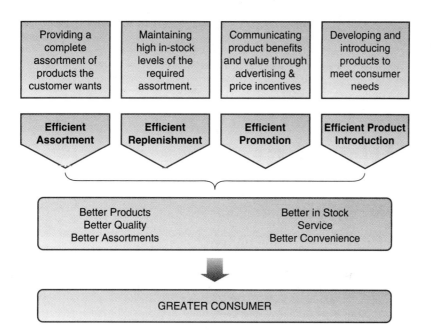

**FIGURE 4.1**  *Impact of ECR on Consumer Satisfaction*

channels, and products. Retailers and suppliers must be patient. Although no true competitive advantage was found, a competitive disadvantage was attributed to those who did not practice ECR. One of the major advantages is the transition from an adversarial relationship to a collaborative retailer–supplier relationship. Innovation and cooperation have improved efficiency and effectiveness to provide a better response to the needs of the ultimate consumer. Figure 4.2 shows the cost savings related to ECR.

In addition to providing customers with a better and more satisfying shopping experience, retailers and their partners accrue a number of financial benefits by:

1. Lowering the cost of goods and damaged goods.
2. Reducing trade and consumer administration expenses and fewer product introduction failures.
3. Selling and buying become more automated with continuous replenishment and electronic data exchange eliminating the need for field personnel.

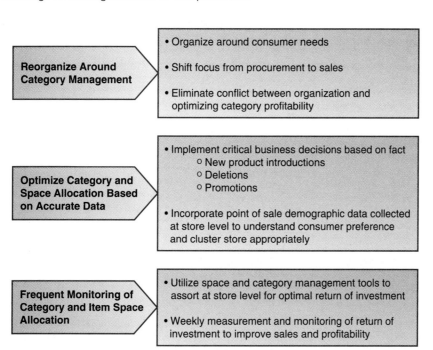

**FIGURE 4.2**  *Cost Savings of ECR*

4. Operating distribution centers, warehouses, and trucks are used more efficiently.

5. Eliminating some of the clerical and accounting personnel.

6. Increasing sales per square foot/linear foot/cubic foot by using automated ordering (Kurt Salmon Associates 1993).

# Efficient Assortment

Creating an **efficient assortment** is a major part of ECR. Efficient assortment maximizes space use and efficiency, including shelf space and storage space, while providing consumer satisfaction. Category management, the development of the systematic consideration of merchandise planning, is the outcome of the efficient assortment initiative. The allocation of shelf space is based on the (1) analysis of both accurate data and POS scan data from the store; (2) store-level sales history, which is adjusted for promotions and seasons; (3) item database, including physical product characteristics, price, and cost information; and (4) point-of-sale consumer identification and demographics, using consumers' zip codes, loyalty card information, and/or credit card information.

Implementing efficient assortments has many benefits, in addition to increased sales and gross margin; however, some are difficult to quantify, such as customer satisfaction and the resulting store loyalty.

# Efficient Replenishment

The purpose of **efficient replenishment** is to jointly manage inventories to streamline the distribution of merchandise and lower warehousing and distribution costs. Retailing success depends on having the right product at the right place at the right time in the right quantities, which is the purpose of efficient replenishment. In addition, by managing inventories, retailers and suppliers reduce warehousing and distribution costs. Efficient replenishment links the customers, retail store, distribution center, corporate headquarters, and supplier into a synchronized system. Information is transferred accurately through the **electronic data interchange (EDI)** system. Merchandise is transferred from the manufacturer to the distribution center, to the store, and finally to the customer (Kurt Salmon Associates 1993).

Much inefficiency is linked to replenishment, including the buildup of inventory in a warehouse or distribution center, which cost the retailer a great deal in terms of labor and potential loss. These inefficiencies include:

1. Excess inventory carrying costs
2. Increased damages
3. Excess administrative costs
4. Highly fluctuating manufacturing schedules

For example, merchandise is pushed into the distribution center when the manufacturer offers the retailer a special price and the retailer purchases additional goods. Merchandise is pulled out of the distribution center by store replenishment orders necessitated by customer purchases. This push-and-pull dynamic causes a lack of synchronization between the buying and selling process. The most efficient way for retailers to maintain cash flow is to pay for merchandise after the merchandise is sold. When retailers warehouse merchandise for a period of time longer than usual, they basically pay "rent" for the space, and their cash flow is diminished. The push dynamic minimizes the cash flow of the retailer, and increases the likelihood of merchandise becoming damaged.

Several initiatives have improved replenishment, including:

1. **Cross-Docking.** Cross-docking occurs when the merchandise is delivered to the distribution center just in time to be sent to the store. The term originally was coined to mean the merchandise crossed the shipping dock from one truck to another without entering the distribution center or warehouse.

2. **Advance Shipping Notices (ASN).** The ASN is a shipping label on the outside of the box with all of the information needed to process the order.

3. **Direct Store Delivery (DSD).** Direct store delivery is very common with certain types of merchandise found in grocery stores, including soft drinks, beer, chips, and snacks. The manufacturer delivers the merchandise directly to the store. The merchandise is not handled by the store personnel.

4. **Computer Assisted Ordering (CAO).** CAO automates the generation of the store replenishment orders and is used extensively in consumer packaged goods. The successful implementation of CAO has four key elements:

   a. Accurate scanning of products at the store level by sales associates

   b. Accurate communication between the database systems used by the retailers and their vendors

   c. Perpetual store inventory system based on accurate scanning

   d. Use of EDI systems and databases provided by the retailer and vendors

# Efficient Promotions

The purpose of **efficient promotions** is to reduce the cost of promotions. The promotion spending mix has dramatically changed since the inception of ECR. In the past, the mix was a combination of advertising, consumer promotion, and trade promotion. This mix continues to change and evolve.

Whereas technology has made many aspects of retailing more efficient and effective, technology has made the implementation and development of promotions more difficult. In the past, the retailing industry focused on print, radio, and television advertising; **trade promotions**; and **customer promotions**. The advent of the digital video recorder (DVR), and the anticipated demise of many forms of print media, including newspapers and magazines, has impacted the success and potential efficiency of these traditional forms of advertisement. In addition, the Internet has changed advertisements—many video clips viewed on the Internet follow a brief, yet required-to-view, advertisement. These changes have forced all of the parties to reevaluate their assessment of efficient promotions.

Trade promotions are expenses paid directly by a manufacturer to a retailer for a merchandising opportunity provided by the retailer. Trade promotions include **slotting allowances** and retailer–specific promotions. A slotting allowance is a fee that suppliers pay retailers for shelf space within a store. Trade promotions have been found to account for

15%–25% of retailers' gross revenue. Suppliers use trade promotions to improve their relationship with retailers and build brand loyalty with the customers, thereby increasing sales. **Forward buying** is a type of trade promotion that adds costs to the distribution process. Forward buying is purchasing large quantities of merchandise when it is offered at a discount by the manufacturer. Retailers then store the merchandise until they need the merchandise in the retail store.

Customer promotions are promotions directed to the customer, including coupons, in-store discounts, and sampling. Between 2004 and 2007, a significant number of shoppers (17%, up from 13%) tried new products on promotion. The majority of those trying new products were under age 55. In 2005, a study of European shoppers found that 69% of shoppers purchase new products or different brands because of a promotional activity.

# Efficient Product Introductions

**Efficient product introductions** aim to increase the success rate of incorporating new products into the merchandising mix by analyzing point-of-sales data on a timely basis. The management of product introductions will lower the number of unsuccessful introductions, and offer products to customers with greater value. New product introductions have two crucial aspects: (1) timing, and (2) innovation. Meeting the real or perceived needs of the customer may determine the eventual success of new products. Many new products are actually extensions of a current brand. These brand extensions may be in the form of flavors, sizes, and/or other attributes. ECR Europe conducted a study of new product introductions; they found that only 2.2% of all new products were actually new, 6.1% were line extensions, and 77% were replicas of other products. Therefore, true innovation represents only a small percentage of new products. Unfortunately, most new products do not survive over a year. Of the truly new products, 43% were failures/near failures within a year, 51% of the line extensions failed within a year, and 77% of the replicated products failed within a year (ECR Europe 1999).

Many retailers, including grocery stores and pet supply stores, offer their customers frequent buyer cards with a bar code. The bar code allows the retailer to add the customer to a database and relate the customer to their home address. The cards also enable retailers to determine how sending promotions to specific zip codes affects their customers' buying habits by tracking the promotion and the resulting purchases. New products may be tested in limited market areas to determine their potential for success. Retailers can also test new private label products and customer satisfaction. The benefits include (1) reducing the failure rate of new products, (2) testing new products in a realistic environment, and (3) determining the likelihood of new product profitability (Kurt Salmon Associates 1993).

# Evolution of Efficient Consumer Response

Category management is at the core of demand management. **Demand management** includes the optimization of assortments, promotions and new product introductions.

The purpose of supply management is to offer the customer the right amount of the right product at the right time in the right place as efficiently as possible. Efficient product replenishment has been the most successful initiative in providing cost savings to retailers and suppliers. The factors enabling this savings is automated ordering, cross-docking, collaboration between suppliers, demand forecasting and production planning. The key factors for implementation are point of sale (POS) data and standardized product delivery package identifications such as RFID.

Technology that enables ECR includes common identification standards, standard electronic messages, and global data synchronization. Technology allows retailers to track sales, track customer preferences, and increase the accuracy of cost accounting. Technology enables companies to get new information about the value chain cost structure.

Collaborative planning and forecasting as well as cost/profit and value measurement enable retailers and suppliers to combine the other features for a comprehensive assessment of ECR. A related initiative is Collaboration, Planning, Forecasting, and Replenishment (CPFR) is a cross-industry initiative designed to improve the relationships between suppliers and retailers. CPFR takes collaboration beyond the past collaborative strategies of **vendor managed inventory (VMI)**, supplier managed inventory, and **continuous replenishment program (CRP)**. CPFR adds the essential component of collaborative planning and forecasting. CPFR assists in helps streamlining the business process in the value chain, but requires a high degree of trust and a measureable improvement in data. Whereas CPFR is a development of the supply side of ECR; **Collaborative Customer Relationship Management (CCRM)** is a development of the demand side. CCRM enables retailers and suppliers to manage all touch points of the customer experience (point of sale, television, radio, call center, e-mail, Internet, etc.). ECR is a retail strategy that is constantly evolving. As technology improves and the relationships between suppliers and retailers become more collaborative, ECR will continue to change.

# Review

A value chain is a flow of processes in which a product gains value (Wikipedia). The management and improvement of the retail value chain has been an evolution of processes and thought. Three major movements within the retail industry have enabled the development of the retail value chain: (1) Quick Response (QR), (2) Kurt Salmon and Associates Efficient Consumer Response (ECR) model of 1992 and (3) Collaboration, Planning, Forecasting, and Replenishment (CPFR) (Finne and Sioven 2009).

Efficient Consumer Response (ECR) drew from best practices in the grocery industry, as well as other industry strategies such as Quick Response (QR) in the general merchandise industry and **Total Quality Management (TQM)** in the manufacturing industry. ECR is a retail management strategy developed in the 1990s for retailers, wholesalers, and suppliers to create and sustain competitive advantage by making the supply chain more competitive and to bring greater value to the grocery consumer.

There are four basic subject areas: (1) efficient store assortments, (2) efficient replenishment, (3) efficient promotions, and (4) efficient product introductions. These initiatives serve to lower the overall costs of business and to improve efficiency by decreasing paperwork and relying instead on technology.

# key terms

# activities

- Prepare a presentation briefly explaining ECR as if you were presenting to a group without a retail background.

- Complete the Harvard Business School case study: Zara: Fast Fashion.

- Watch the Harvard Business School video or CD-ROM, Zara: Fast Fashion.

# discussion questions

1. Define value chain management.
2. Apply the value chain management concept to retailing.
3. How has the relationship between suppliers and retailers changed?
4. List the four key attributes of ECR.
5. List the five guiding principles of ECR.
6. How has ECR saved grocery retailers money?
7. How does ECR create greater consumer satisfaction?
8. Explain the purpose of efficient assortment.
9. List inefficiencies in the supply chain during replenishment.
10. List the technological changes in retailing that improved the process of replenishment.
11. Discuss the challenges in developing efficient promotions.
12. Discuss the benefits of testing new products prior to introduction. Define trade promotion.
13. Define slotting allowance.
14. What are the two crucial aspects of new product introduction?
15. List the benefits of ECR.

# references, resources, web sites, and recommended readings

- Bhulai, S. 1997. Efficient Consumer Response. http://www.math.vu.nl/

- Dess, G., G. T. Lumpkin, and A. Eisner. 2006. *Strategic Management*, 2nd Ed. New York: McGraw-Hill Irwin.

- ECR Europe. 2001. *A guide to CPFR implementation*. Spain: ECR Europe and Accenture.

- Finne, S., and H. Sivonen. 2009. *The retail value chain*. London, UK and Philadelphia, USA: Kogan Page Ltd.

- Frozen Food Digest. 1997. Market study results released: new product introduction success, failure rates analyzed. *Frozen Food Digest* (July 1), http://www.allbusiness.com/marketing/market-research/631186-1.html (accessed March 9, 2009).

- Hashmi, K. 2003. Introduction and implementation of Total Quality Management (TQM). *iSixSigma.com*. October 8. http://www.isixsigma.com/library/content/c031008a.asp (accessed March 17, 2009).

- Klaassen, A. 2006. *Marketers lose confidence in TV advertising: 78% say effectiveness is diminishing: Clutter, DVRs to blame.* March 22. New York: Ad Age.

- Kracklauer, A., Mills, D. Q., and D. Seifert. 2010. *Collaborative Customer Relationship Management.* New York: Springer Berlin Heidelberg.

- Kurt Salmon Associates, Inc. 1993. *Efficient consumer response. Joint industry project on efficient consumer response.* Washington, DC: Food Marketing Institute.

- Kurt Salmon Associates, Inc. 1997. *Quick response: Meeting customer need.* Atlanta, GA: Kurt Salmon Associates.

- Masters, K. 2007. *In the age of TiVO, advertisers scramble to keep up.* NPR. http://www.npr.org/s.php?sld=10190951&m=1 (accessed March 15, 2009).

- McKinnon, A. 1996. *The development of retail logistics in the UK.* A position paper. UK Technology Foresight. http://www.sml.hw.ac.uk/logistics/pdf/RetLogES.pdf (accessed March 15, 2009).

- Porter, M. 1985. *Competitive Advantage: Creating and Sustaining Superior Performance.* New York: Free Press.

- Schiebel, W. 2000. The value chain analysis of ECR Europe: Interpreting a system innovation in supply chains. *Proceedings of the Fourth International Conference on Chain Management in Agribusiness and the Food Industry. May 25–26.* 645–652. Wageningen: Wageningen University Press.

- Trade Promotion Management. http://www.wipro.com (accessed March 3, 2009).

# CATEGORY MANAGEMENT CYCLES

On completion of this chapter, the student will be able to:

- Explain the eight-step category management cycle.
- Draw a customer decision-making tree.
- Explain the levels of a category, and the four basic category roles.
- Explain the relationship between assessment and the score card.
- Define the category strategies.
- List the category tactics.
- Understand the challenges of in-store execution.
- Explain the category review process.

5

# Introduction

Category management is a method of managing retailing to accommodate increasingly complex and changing customer demographics with a clear, distinct, and achievable plan. Category management enables retailers to use all available resources—including technology, collaborative business relationships, organization structure, assessment tools, strategy, and business processes—to achieve retail success. This chapter discusses the category management cycle developed by the Partnering Group.

# Category Management Cycle

The Partnering Group identified two core components of category management: (1) **strategy**, and (2) business process. Strategy refers to the retailer's overall business strategy. The business process is the day-to-day work required to achieve the strategy, including a structured set of activities designed to achieve a specific result. The Partnering Group developed the Eight Stage Category Management Process, cited by many as a best practice in category management. This eight-stage category management cycle, Figure 5.1, has remained standard in the industry, although other cycles have been published in retailing literature and developed by category management teams. This book describes this eight-stage cycle and its adaptations. The stages in the original cycle developed by the Partnering Group are: (1) **category definition**, (2) **category role**, (3) **category assessment**, (4) **category scorecard** or performance measures, (5) **category strategies**, (6) **category tactics**, (7) implementation or execution, and (8) **category review** (Partnering Group 1995). Although the stages in the cycle are discussed separately, many steps in this cycle overlap.

**FIGURE 5.1** *Category Management Cycle*
(Courtesy of The Partnering Group)

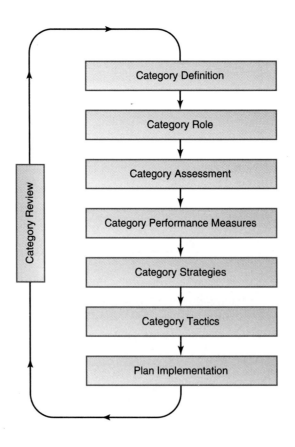

# Category Definition

**Category definition** is the first step of the cycle. Category definition is critical to the retailer's differentiation strategy because the way retailers determine the segments within a category ultimately impacts the retailer's market position (ECR Europe 2000). Category definition defines and segments the category according to the customers' wants and needs, determined by first preparing a customer decision-making tree and then the SKUs in the category. To accurately define a category, retailers must seek information from at least two sources: (1) a review of the current definition used by the retailer, competition, vendors, and customer; and (2) customer behavior research. The first is fairly easy to assess through observation. The second is a little more difficult, but can be assessed by observing the customer shop, conducting exit interviews, and analyzing their **market basket**; this information is often gathered from POS data, loyalty cards, etc.

A category is defined as a distinct, manageable group of products and/or services that customers perceive to be interrelated and or substitutable in meeting their needs (Partnering Group 1995). Each type of retailer defines a category based on the company's product assortment. For example, a pet store may define categories such as (1) fish, (2) dogs, (3) cats, (4) small pets, (5) reptiles, (6) birds, and (7) wild birds. Book stores have categories such as (1) children's books, (2) romance novels, (3) business books, (4) religious books, and (5) magazines.

Typical categories in grocery stores are: soft drinks, baking goods, dairy, bottled water, etc. Each category may include several types of products. For instance, the bottled water category includes distilled water, domestic spring water, imported water, mineral water, flavored waters, and vitamin waters. The containers include plastic bottles and glass bottles, and many sizes ranging up to five-gallon bottles. Water is a distinct manageable group of products that customers see as substitutable. When a retailer defines a category such as bottled water, they include all of the options they sell and determine whether the assortment meets the wants and needs of the customer. To determine the wants and needs of the customer, retailers develop a **customer decision-making tree** (Figure 5.2) that allows them to determine how categories are defined based on the customer's behavior and decision-making process. The customer's actions and decisions should lead the process. The example in the customer decision-making tree shows how a customer makes a decision in regard to soft drinks, a category typically found in a grocery store, convenience store, or mass merchandiser. Once a customer decides to purchase a soft drink upon entering the aisle where the category is located, the customer begins to make decisions based on brand, caloric value, size, and container type. Although the customer routinely makes decisions, he or she is rarely cognizant of this very fast-paced process. However, retailers must analyze the decision-making process in order to accurately define the category.

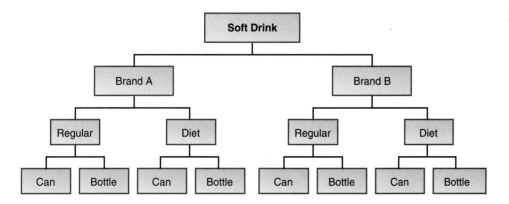

**FIGURE 5.2** *Customer Decision-Making Tree*

FIGURE 5.3 *Levels of Categories* (Courtesy of The Partnering Group)

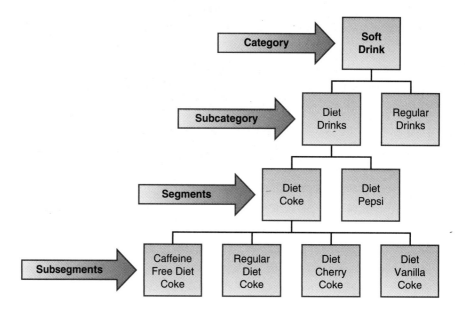

Based on the decision-making tree, retailers develop **subcategories**, then segments, and then subsegments. This is an important step in the category management process. Breaking the category down enables the retailer and category managers to focus on smaller data sets for a more in-depth analysis. As a category is broken down into **segments** and **subsegments** and finally products, each level becomes more discrete and more easily assessed. A category definition must be defined to at least four levels: category, subcategory, segment, and subsegment (ECR Europe 2000). The segments may then be based on the brand, and the subsegments based on the **brand extensions** within the segments (Figure 5.3). Brand extensions are the addition of a new product to an already-established line of products under the same name. For instance, Cherry Coke and Vanilla Coke are brand extensions of Coke.

Another example of segmentation is the category of dog products at a pet store; the subcategories include food, grooming, apparel, and treats and biscuits (PetsMart.com). The segments of dog food are defined by price, lifestyle, pet size, special features, style, or flavor. The segments are then defined into subsegments such as dry or canned foods.

The retailer determines the manner in which the category is defined. A clear understanding of the customer's needs, buying behavior, and the interrelationships between the product attributes such as the choices within a subsegment, is essential for success in the category management process (ECR Europe 2000). Over time, retailers may change the way the category is defined. However, the definition is always determined by the way the customer shops the category. When a retailer seeks to redefine a category, they use customer research, which impacts the category definition and customer decision-making tree. One of the challenges in category definition is focusing on the customer's behavior rather than the vendor's definition. For instance, when a customer plans to make banana pudding, the retailer must plan in the same way a customer thinks. The customer is thinking of the ingredients in the recipe: bananas, milk, pudding mix, and vanilla wafers. A retailer focused on the customer will place pudding mix and vanilla wafers in a display beside the bananas in the produce department. In a vendor's definition, the vanilla wafers should be in the cookie category and the pudding in a baking category. Changing the way a category is defined impacts the retailer in the merchandising of products within the category. In examples like banana pudding, retailers often include products in two or more categories and locations. The next step is determining the role a category plays within a retailer.

# Category Role

The second step is determining the **category role**. The category role is determined by the priority of importance of different categories in a retailer's business. The role of a category differs widely depending on the retail channel. There are four basic category roles: destination, **routine, occasional/seasonal**, and **convenience**. The destination role, such as milk in a grocery store or gas/soft drinks in a convenience store (1) defines the image of the retailer, (2) is important to the target shopper, (3) leads all categories in terms of sales growth, and (4) uses a high percentage of the retailer's resources, including personnel, space, and inventory investment. The routine category provides a balance between value, growth and profit; often they are products that customers purchase routinely, such as paper towels or toilet tissue in a grocery store. The seasonal category is important to the consumer by providing part of their regular grocery needs. For example, Easter baskets and Easter supplies are examples of products in the seasonal category for most stores. The occasional/seasonal category may serve as a **destination category** on a seasonal basis. The fourth role is the convenience role, which allows the customer to purchase within the category on a less frequent basis, but gives a retailer the image of being a one-stop shop and an opportunity for profit growth (ECR Europe 2000). For instance, the role of the category of soft drinks in a convenience store is very different than its role in a grocery store. In a convenience store, soft drinks products serve in a **destination role**. In a grocery store, soft drinks serve in a routine or convenience role.

As retailers begin to assign roles to each category, they review the baseline data. The baseline data enables retailers to review the historical information and forecast into the future. After establishing the projections for category performance, the category management team can realistically assign category roles. This stage is important to the category management cycle; it enables retailers to (1) assign placement within the store of the category, (2) project retail sales, (3) allocate personnel resources, and (4) satisfy the customer. When determining the role, retailers must understand the (1) customers' shopping behavior, (2) overall market, (3) competition, (4) retailer's financial status, and (5) customer demographics. Each role is discussed in more detail in Chapter 6.

# Category Performance Assessment

The next step in a retailer's strategy is **category assessment**. This step enables retailers to determine opportunities for improving the category's business by identifying opportunity gaps in sales, profit, and stock turn (Singh and Blattberg 2001). This step allows the retailer to assess the current status so that they may develop goals and objectives in the next step. When completing this assessment, the retailer typically asks the following questions:

- Who are the retailer's target shoppers, and is the retailer reaching them?
- Why are the target shoppers a total store opportunity for the retailer?
- Who is the retailer's competition for target shoppers?
- What opportunities exist to improve position against key competitors?
- What are the strategic categories in the market, and for the retailer's target shoppers?
- How should the retailer allocate category roles at a cross-category level, and then prioritize resources in line with category opportunities?
- What are the demographics of the segments?

- Who are the key competitors in the category?
- How are the segments performing?
- Which products help build traffic, incidence, transaction, and profit?
- What are the key tactical drivers that may impact segment performance? (ECR Europe 2000)

Category assessment focuses on research and analysis of the category's performance. This is where the retailer decides whether the category matches the target customer by providing the brands and segments they seek, and how well the retailer is performing. While completing this step, the relationship between the retailer and vendors is extremely important. They must be able to share information, including customer demographic and lifestyle data, syndicated data, retail space allocation or planograming data, brand data, category trends, market share data, competitor analysis, data indicating the effectiveness of promotions, cost data, and profit data (Singh and Blattberg 2001). The assessment stage is discussed in further detail in Chapter 6.

# Category Scorecard or Performance Measures

The next step in the category management cycle is the category scorecard (see Figure 5.4), or performance measure. This is when retailers set proposed goals in regard to sales, stock turn, profit, gross margin return on investment, and other measures of productivity for the role of each category. When a retailer develops a scorecard, they must: (1) set up the criteria for the guiding principles, (2) design a system to generate and manage the scorecard measures, (3) acquire the technology necessary to maintain the scorecard, and (4) propose incentives for both retail employees and vendors upon achievement of the goals established by the scorecard (Partnering Group 1995). The guiding principles of a category scorecard should be:

1. Relevant to the corporate strategy
2. Balanced between the retailer and vendors
3. Encompass the entire business activity of the category
4. Standardized across business units for ease of comparison across the retailer's business

| Consumer: | | | |
|---|---|---|---|
| Number of Items in Market Basket | _____ | _____ | _____ |
| Dollar Value of Market Basket | _____ | _____ | _____ |
| Market Share | _____ | _____ | _____ |
| Sales | _____ | _____ | _____ |
| Sales/Sq. Ft. Per Week | _____ | _____ | _____ |
| Gross Profit | _____ | _____ | _____ |
| Gross Margin % | _____ | _____ | _____ |
| Gross Profit/Sq. Ft. Per Week | _____ | _____ | _____ |
| Day of Supply | _____ | _____ | _____ |
| Stock Turns | _____ | _____ | _____ |
| GMROII or ROA | _____ | _____ | _____ |

**FIGURE 5.4** *Typical Scorecard*

5. Timely; the scorecard is relevant only if the data is timely
6. Understandable by all stakeholders
7. Accurate; the scorecard must accurately assess the performance of the category

The scorecard compares the actual measures versus the target measures. For instance, one goal may be having a product from the category in every 10 percent of all market baskets. Retailers analyze the POS data to determine the actual percentage of market baskets having products from the category. They also review the financial data related to the category, including sales, gross margin, profit, and return on assets. Finally, they determine whether retailers have the proposed market share of sales, which are syndicated data aids in this analysis. In addition to measuring the financial data, they analyze the merchandising data, including inventory (days of supply), out of stocks (OOS), and stock turn or turnover.

The next step is determining the strategy for each category. However, before the category strategy is determined, the mission and strategy of the retailer must be reviewed. Understanding a retailer's overall mission and strategy is key to creating an executable plan. Ultimately, the strategies developed for the categories must be consistent with the department and the retailer's corporate strategy. When assessing the retailer's mission and strategy, several basic questions need to be answered:

- What is the image of the retailer? This includes price, assortment, quality, consistency, and customer service.
- What are the key performance measures, as determined by the retailer and retail analysts? These include market share, operating expense as a percentage of sales, sales, gross margin, net profit, return on assets, stock turn, GMROII, and OOS.

# Category Strategies

The fifth step in the **category cycle** is category strategy—the process where strategies are developed to deliver on the category role and category scorecard. This stage is very important because the strategies also impact the choice of tactics in developing the category. The development of category strategies has five basic drivers:

1. Total number of shopping trips
2. Percentage of shopping trips that contain the category
3. Value transaction of the market basket
4. Gross margin
5. Actual profit (ECR Europe 2000)

Retailers and vendors assess several criteria when choosing the appropriate strategy. The category management team seeks to focus on growth and profit by using one of the following strategies:

1. **Traffic building:** Merchandise that has a high market share, is frequently purchased, and is a high percentage of overall sales. This strategy focuses on driving customer traffic into the store and to the aisle where the merchandise is located. Examples of traffic-building merchandise include: soft drinks, toilet paper, and paper towels.
2. **Transaction building:** Merchandise with higher dollar sales and is often an impulse purchase. This strategy focuses on increasing the size of the average transaction within a category, aisle, or total store. Examples of transaction building are the merchandise used in

an in-store cooking demonstration in a grocery store, merchandise for a party, or merchandise for a trip to the beach.

3. **Profit contributing:** Merchandise with a higher gross margin and higher stock turn. This strategy focuses on the ability to generate profit. Examples of this strategy include any product with a high profit margin, such as a soft drink from a fountain or fashion clothing.

4. **Cash generating:** Frequently purchased merchandise with a higher stock turn. Examples include milk, eggs, meat, and vegetables.

5. **Excitement creating:** Merchandise that is often an impulse purchase, lifestyle oriented, or seasonal. This merchandise creates a sense of urgency or opportunity to the customer. Examples include a "one-time purchase," holiday decorations, the most popular children's toy for a holiday season, or a new computer game.

6. **Image enhancing:** Merchandise that enhances the image of the retailer based on the retailer's total image, whether it is as a one-stop retailer or the retailer that has the newest and trendiest merchandise. This includes highly promoted merchandise, impulse merchandise, unique merchandise, or seasonal merchandise. Examples are the Wii console and games.

7. **Turf defending:** Merchandise that positions the category to appeal to the customer in comparison with the competition. This merchandise is used by the retailer to draw their traditional customer base. Examples may include private label food and pharmacy brands (Partnering Group 1995).

Category strategies are discussed in more detail in Chapter 7. Once the strategies are decided for each category, the tactics or actions are chosen to help the retailer achieve the strategic goal (Partnering Group 1995).

# Category Tactics

The goal of category tactics is to choose a specific action to achieve a specific strategy. The six areas of tactics are: (1) assortment, (2) pricing, (3) promotion, (4) merchandising, (5) service, and (6) micro-marketing. Figure 5.5 shows the six category tactics. This process must include all

**FIGURE 5.5** *Category Tactics*

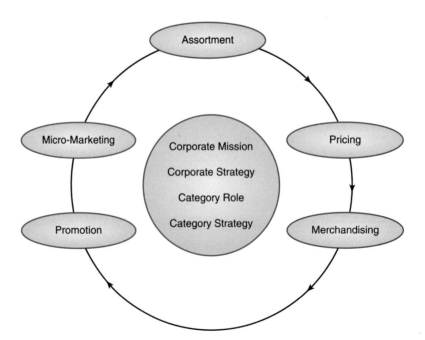

personnel, including category management, store operations, merchandising, and regional directors/store managers. Each is important in determining the appropriate tactic for success. The store operations personnel determine the impact and/or timing of the store roll-out of new products, as well help the category management team with timing new product introductions and **delists**, promotional calendars, and merchandising recommendations. A delist is a list of products eliminated from the assortment. The merchandising team helps determine the appropriate timing for a change in merchandising. The regional directors and store managers are critical to the success of any program. If the retailer wants to make any changes, their buy-in to the change is crucial.

# Plan Execution or Implementation

The next step in the process is **plan execution**, or implementation. This is the step in which the retailer sets the merchandise in the store based on a careful analysis of the category. All other steps are fruitless without the successful implementation of the planogram developed through this planning and analysis. In addition to making decisions related to the appropriate placement of merchandise, retailers must also trust the store employees to ensure that the merchandising has been implemented. A great planogram is successful only when implemented correctly and on time. Unfortunately, this is where the category management cycle often fails. For the successful execution of a planogram, several components of the execution process should:

1. Be consistent with the retailer's overall strategy
2. Be based on the relevant performance measures
3. Agree with the allocation of resources provided by the retailer (shelf space, promotion activity, personnel, fixture type)
4. Positively impact other categories within the retailer's merchandise mix (Partnering Group 1995)

Prior to in-store execution, many steps within the process should be developed:

1. Notify in-store personnel of any major changes, including the moving of fixtures, change of fixtures, or relocating categories of merchandise.
2. Involve all management personnel involved in the decision-making process.
3. Notify all personnel involved in the assessment of the store's productivity in regard to disruptions of service or cost associated with the execution.

Once the implementation begins, first test the new planogram in a number of "test" stores to ensure the planogram is operational. Check the stores to ensure compliance with the new planograms. After the planogram is operational and has had time to impact sales, check the productivity data (ECR Europe 2000).

The major steps in execution are shown in Figure 5.6. The figure shows the approximate time each step takes and which steps will happen simultaneously.

# Category Review

This is the final step in the category management process—but in the terms of a cycle, the plan review can also be viewed as the beginning step. The dynamics of a category, and the innovations within the merchandise offerings, determine the frequency of a plan review. However, all plans must be reviewed on a periodic and consistent basis.

**FIGURE 5.6** *Execution*

| | MONTH 1 | | | | MONTH 2 | | | | MONTH 3 | | | |
|---|---|---|---|---|---|---|---|---|---|---|---|---|
| | 1 | 2 | 3 | 4 | 1 | 2 | 3 | 4 | 1 | 2 | 3 | 4 |
| Review Data | | | | | | | | | | | | |
| Finalize Assortment Decision | | | | | | | | | | | | |
| Develop New Planograms | | | | | | | | | | | | |
| Collect New POS Data | | | | | | | | | | | | |
| Analyze Data | | | | | | | | | | | | |
| Update Scorecard | | | | | | | | | | | | |

The plan review is an opportunity for the category management team, including the retailer and vendors, to review all of the performance measurements to determine whether the category is meeting the goals set in the category scorecard. Typical data used to measure success includes POS data, syndicated data, and consumer research. Data includes yearly sales, profit, margin, GMROII, shopper loyalty data, record of OOS, and turnover. This step in the cycle can be either the beginning or end of the cycle, depending on whether retailers are starting a new category or reviewing an existing one. This cycle continues to the first step and enables retailers to maintain a productive category.

A cycle is simply a tool to allow persons engaged in an activity to develop a timeline and insure all of the activities are included in the plan. No cycle is perfect for everyone or totally inclusive. However, a cycle is an opportunity for all of the stakeholders to review the process and refine the cycle to meet the needs of a given activity. The original category management cycle, or the many adaptations conceived afterwards, assist in the implementation of category management, and hopefully a successful implementation.

# Review

Category management is a method of managing retailing to accommodate increasingly complex and changing demographics with a clear, distinct, and achievable plan. The Partnering Group identified two core components of category management: strategy and business process. The stages in the original cycle developed by the Partnering Group are: (1) category definition, (2) category role, (3) category assessment, (4) category scorecard or performance measures, (5) category strategies, (6) category tactics, (7) implementation or execution, and (8) category review (Partnering Group 1995). Category definition defines and segments the category according to the customers' wants and needs. The category role is determined by the priority of importance of different categories in a retailer's business. Category assessment enables retailers to determine opportunities for improving the category's business by identifying opportunity gaps in sales, profit, and stock turn (Singh and Blattberg 2001). Category scorecard or performance measure is where retailers set proposed goals in regard to sales, stock turn, profit, gross margin return on investment, and other measures of productivity for the role of the category. Category strategy is the step in the process where strategies are developed to deliver on the category role and category scorecard. The goal of category tactics is to choose a specific action to achieve a specific strategy. Execution or implementation is the step in which the retailer sets the merchandise in the store based on a careful analysis of the category. The plan review is an opportunity for the category management team, including the retailer and vendors, to review all of the performance measurements to determine whether the category is meeting the goals set in the category scorecard.

# key terms

# activities

For each of the next chapters, you will build upon the following activity:

- Choose a category of merchandise in a store. Review (photograph) the planograms of the products at two different retailers. Answer the following questions:
  - How does each retailer define the category?

- What are the products in this category?
- Review (photograph) the planograms of the products at three different retailers.

- How do you think each retailer developed the customer decision-making tree for the category? Draw a customer decision-making tree for each retailer.

# discussion questions

1. Describe the eight-step category management cycle.
2. Discuss how a customer decision-making tree can help a retailer define a category.
3. What are the different levels of a category? Why is it important to differentiate these levels?
4. What are the four basic category roles? Give an example for each of them.

5. What is the relationship between assessment and the score card?
6. How do category tactics interact with category strategies?
7. Give three challenges of in-store execution.

# references, resources, web sites, and recommended readings

- ACNielsen. http://www2.acnielsen.com/pubs/2004_q3_ci_consumer.shtml/
- ECR Europe. 2000. *The essential guide to day-to-day category management.*
- Partnering Group. 1995. Category Management Report. *Joint Industry Project on Efficient Consumer Response.* Washington, DC: Food Marketing Institute.
- Partnering Group. http://www.partneringgroup.com/
- PetSmart. http://www.Petsmart.com/
- Singh, J. and R. Blattberg. 2001. *New generation category management.* Category Management, Inc. London: Datamonitor PLC.

# CATEGORY
## ROLE

**LEARNING GOALS**

On completion of this chapter, the student will be able to:

- Describe each of the four category roles.
- Discuss the information needed to determine the category roles.
- Develop baseline information for the category role.
- Explain the importance of analysis of the market as it pertains to the category role.
- Explain the importance of analysis of the competition as it pertains to the category role.
- Explain the importance of analysis of the internal financials as it pertains to the category role.
- Explain the importance of analysis of the shoppers as it pertains to the category role.
- Explain the importance of analysis of the store conditions as it pertains to the category role.
- Assess the category role.

6

# Introduction

Stew Leonard's is a small chain of supermarkets in Connecticut and New York. The typical store attracts customers from a wider geographic area than a typical supermarket. Customers are willing to drive longer distances because of the store's innovative in-store marketing and customer service policy etched into a three-ton rock at each store's entrance:

1. The customer is always right.
2. If the customer is ever wrong, re-read #1. (www.stewleonards.com)

Stew Leonard's philosophy epitomizes one of the basic tenets of category management: You must market to the customer. In addition, retailers must remember that there is not just one type of customer for the retailer or the category. Category management involves both **supply management** as well as **logistics** and front-of-the-store activities by increasing store traffic or the likelihood that customers will shop a certain category. To be successful, retailers must determine the role each category plays, develop strategies to positively enhance retail sales, and successfully and consistently execute the plan.

# Understanding the Category Role

The first step in understanding category management is to begin to understand the role that each product within an assortment or category plays. The customer ultimately decides on the role. As a retailer begins to understand the customer, they begin to understand how to successfully compete for the customer. The basic steps are to: (1) determine who shops the retailer, (2) analyze the customers and their shopping category, (3) determine whether the target customer of the category aligns with the retailer's target customer, (4) assess the impact of the category on other categories, (5) determine the value of the customer to the retailer, and (6) determine the critical buying decisions of the customer when choosing a retailer, category, or product. All of these steps are related to understanding how the customer relates to the category and retailer.

# Baseline for Category Role

To better understand the category role, it is essential to create a baseline of information about the customer, retailer, and market. There are five major steps to creating baseline information:

1. Analysis of market
2. Analysis of competition
3. Analysis of internal financials

4. Analysis of shoppers
5. Analysis of store conditions

There are many ways to gather baseline information, including external sources such as demographics data, traffic data, lifestyle data, and syndicated data. There are also many forms of **internal POS** data, including customer loyalty data and internal financial data. The third source of data is observation of the retail store, the customer, and the competition.

# Analysis of Market

Retailers collect data from all of these sources to analyze the market. For instance, when a retailer begins to develop a plan for a new store, they may begin with the demographic data or data related to the quantitative elements of the population they serve. **Demographic data** includes age, race/ethnic group, income, and size of family and/or household. This data is available through the U.S. Census Bureau as well as many private providers such as Nielsen Claritas.

**Traffic data** is available through the city or state highway departments. This data shows the number of automobiles that pass by a retail site. Many retailers determine their locations based on the number of automobiles or the proximity of the bus route when determining the viability of a shopping center or complex. **Lifestyle data** includes information about a family's life stage; for example, a young family shops differently than an older, retired couple.

The market includes all potential customers within a geographic area. Retailers often look at their markets as all households within a specified radius of their stores or within a driving time from the customer's home to the retailer. Retailers then review the zip code areas to determine the demographic or lifestyle data of the potential customers. After a careful review, retailers focus their marketing efforts on the customers suiting their target customer profile.

# Analysis of Competition

The competition includes all the retailers that offer similar products for sale. For instance, mass merchandisers, convenience stores, and grocery stores offer similar products for sale in many categories. One type of data used to assess the competition is syndicated data. **Syndicated data** compiles POS data from many retailers in a single market, allowing a number of retailer subscribers to analyze their sales of a given product to that of their competitors. Another method used by many retailers is the "store visit" to their stores and their competitors. Retailers at all levels often visit their competitors' stores to view their offerings, prices, and customer service. Often the district, regional, and national directors of a retail company also visit their own stores to complete a self-assessment to compare their stores with their competitors.

# Analysis of Internal Financials

Internal data includes POS data, customer loyalty data, and productivity data, including profit margin, distribution costs, and selling costs. All of these sources work together to compile a more complete perspective of a retailer, the categories within the retailer, and finally the product and how the category contributes to the overall success of the retailer. In the final analysis, the retailer determines how much the customer spends, how frequently they shop, and the categories from which they purchase.

# Analysis of Shoppers

Retailers must determine who shops in their store and why. Is the retailer's proposed target customer actually shopping at the retailer? If so, what are they buying? If not, why not? What are the customers actually buying, and from which categories? How does the shopper affect other categories by increasing or decreasing the sales within other categories? There are several research methods to determine whether a retailer is reaching the target customer. Retailers may examine the POS data to determine the contents of their market basket. A market basket includes all of the merchandise purchased at a single time. For instance, the retailer may analyze all market baskets with a greeting card to find similarities and differences, i.e., persons buying greeting cards may also purchase a bakery cake, ice cream, and candles or wine, cheese, and cocktail napkins. Each market basket has a greeting card; however, the profile of the celebration is different based on the other products in the basket. When a customer uses a frequent buyer card, retailers use a **customer relationship management (CRM)** or customer loyalty database to match their purchases with the customer's zip code. This data is known as **geo-demographic data**. Geo-demographic data includes the geographic location as determined by their zip code plus the demographic data from the U.S. Census Bureau data associated with the zip code. Retailers may also conduct exit interviews as someone leaves the store. They can also watch customers as they shop, or set up a test store and analyze the behavior of the customers. Retailers compare the target customer in a store to national demographic patterns to understand the shopping behavior of their customers, and then plan their assortment and retail strategy to best meet the needs of the customer base.

There are two basic theories about customers and retailing, both of which explain the importance of customers and product assortments. The first and oldest is **Pareto's rule**. Pareto's 80:20 rule says that 20% of a retailer's customers make 80% of the purchases in a retail store, and the reverse is true; 80% of a retailer's customers make only 20% of your sales. This means that you must focus on serving the 20% very well and maintain them as a customer, while providing the necessary service to the remainder.

The second is the **Long Tail** (Figure 6.1), coined by Chris Anderson (2008). This concept explains frequency distribution with a long tail. The theory states that it is possible for businesses to sell many products at a small volume to realize significant profit. This is the complete opposite strategy of most mass merchandisers that adopt the strategy of selling large volumes of a

**FIGURE 6.1** *The Long Tail*

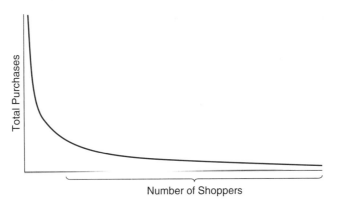

reduced number of popular items. Customers who purchase a large number of different "non-popular" items are called the Long Tail.

Understanding customer behavior is very important because retailers must correctly identify the target customer before planning their strategies and tactics to be successful. Retailers must then ensure that the product developed for the customer meets the needs of the target market. The retail channel or retail format should be the preferred provider of the product. The retailer can then determine the importance of the shopper to the retailer. Upon determining the importance, the retailer may then tailor the strategy: price, assortment, or level of customer service to the importance of the customer.

# Analysis of Store Condition

The fifth step is to analyze the store conditions. These steps may include all aspects of store operations including, but not limited to:

1. Store management
2. Building compliance with corporate standard
3. Maintenance
4. Safety and security
5. Parking
6. Store location
7. Shopping center
8. Movement of population in regard to the location of the shopping center

The management of the store impacts all aspects of the selling environment, including assortment, customer service, safety and security, and check-out efficiency and effectiveness. A poorly maintained store negatively impacts sales and motivates customers to seek alternatives. Customers generally expect a large and/or convenient parking facility with adequate safety and security. The popularity of a shopping center or location will shift as the population shifts. All of these factors should be considered in developing a baseline for a category role.

# Category Roles

There are four basic category roles: destination, routine, occasional/seasonal, and convenience. When a category serves as a **destination** role, the customer enters the retailer to buy the products in that category. For instance, in a grocery store, **destination categories** are bread, meat, dairy, and produce. Because they are destination categories, the merchandise is usually located on the perimeter of the store layout. A destination category in one retail format is not the same as another. For instance, compare grocery stores and convenience stores. In convenience stores soft drinks is a destination category, whereas in a grocery store they may be an occasional or routine role. A destination category: (1) defines the image of the retailer; (2) is very important to the target customer; (3) leads the other categories in sales, market share, customer satisfaction, and service; and (4) consumes a larger percentage of the retailer's resources such as personnel and technology (Partnering Group 1995). The location of the destination categories may be either around the perimeter of the store or in the center of an aisle. The Food Marketing Institute (FMI) classifies products by frequency of purchase and the number of households purchasing a good (penetration). A destination item has both high penetration and high frequency, and is noted as a **staple product** by FMI. Frequency is defined by the average number of times per year a category is purchased. Penetration is the percentage of households purchasing within a category. Figure 6.2 shows how penetration and frequency impact the role of the category.

The second role is the **routine category**; the customer routinely purchases in this category on a consistent basis. For instance, a routine category in a grocery store may be pet products. The customer does not enter the store to purchase pet products, but on a routine basis buys dog treats, dog or cat food, or cat litter. A routine category: (1) defines the retailer as a store of choice by providing products routinely sought by the customer, (2) assists in building the image of the retailer as delivering value to the customer, (3) delivers profit and cash flow through sales, and (4) delivers overall growth to the retailer (Partnering Group 1995). FMI would classify routine products as those with a high frequency of purchase and low penetration of households; this is a **niche product**.

The third role is the **occasional** or **seasonal category**. The customer purchases on a sporadic basis or only during certain seasons. Examples include Halloween, Easter, Christmas, and Cinco de Mayo. Many mass merchandisers now have "seasonal" aisles to serve these categories which change based on the season. The other type of categories that serve in this role

**FIGURE 6.2**  *Market Penetration Versus Visit Frequencies*

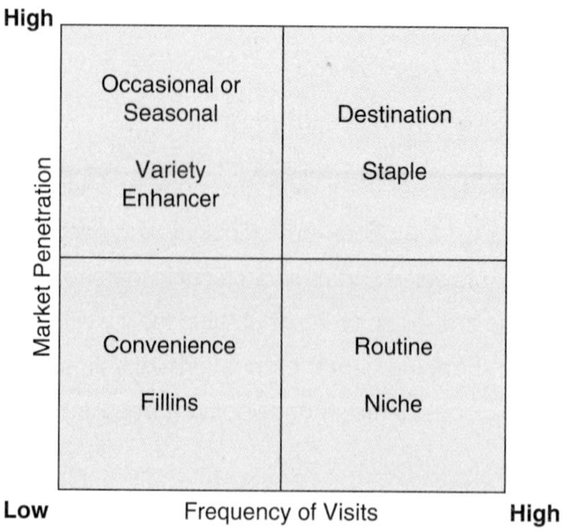

are the products that customers purchase only occasionally, such as cleaning products in a grocery store. An occasional or seasonal category: (1) assists the retailer in meeting the expectations of customers seeking seasonal and occasional products, (2) ensures the image of providing retail value to the target customer, and (3) delivers profit and cash flow (Partnering Group 1995). FMI classifies this product as a **variety enhancer**—products with high penetration in households, but purchased infrequently.

The fourth role is the **convenience category**. Customers purchase these products infrequently, and are important only when the customer buys them. Examples include shoe care products, candy, and hardware. Customers generally do not routinely purchase black shoe polish, candy, or picture-hanging hooks; however, if a mass merchandiser does not have the product available when they seek it, the retailer's image as a store for one-stop shopping is diminished. The convenience category (1) ensures the retailer's image as a one-stop shopping experience, and (2) assists in providing profit margin (Partnering Group 1995). The products with low penetration and low frequency are noted as **fill-ins** by FMI.

The motivation of a customer to purchase a product influences the role or classification of a product. To understand the category role, you must first know the customer:

1. Who shops the retailer?
2. How satisfied are customers with the shopping experience?
3. What is the image of the retailer?
4. Who shops the category?
5. How does the category target customer align with the retailers' target customer?
6. How can this category affect other categories?
7. What is the value of this customer to the retailer?
8. What are the critical buying decisions?
9. Are there other ways to analyze data?
10. What are the significant trends affecting the category?
11. How does cross-merchandising affect the category's role?

The role of a given product changes depending on the retail channel. For instance, in Bath and Body Works, lotion is a destination item, soap is a routine product, gift baskets are occasional or seasonal products, and lip gloss is a convenience product. When you change to another channel such as a mass merchandiser, lotion becomes a routine, occasional/seasonal, or even a convenience product. Roles depend on the image of the retailer and the retail channel and the customers' perceptions of the retailer. Figure 6.3 summarizes the four roles. Although each role is important to the retailer, products serving in the destination role define the retailer and may command the greatest attention. The routine role is also important by assisting the retailer in adding overall growth by providing the customer with products they routinely purchase. The occasional role is important because it provides opportunities to increase the profit margin and cash flow. Finally, the convenience role primarily helps maintain the retailer's image as a one-stop shopping experience.

# Assessing the Role

To ensure that the correct role is assigned to a category, an assessment must be implemented. Retailers begin by identifying the **strengths, weaknesses, threats, and opportunities (SWOT)** of each category. **SWOT** is an analysis of the internal and external environment during

| CATEGORY ROLES | | | |
|---|---|---|---|
| **Destination** | **Routine** | **Occasional or Seasonal** | **Convenience** |
| 1. Defines the image of the retailer | 1. Defines the retailer as a store of choice by providing products routinely sought by the customer | 1. Assists the retailer in meeting the expectations of customers seeking seasonal and occasional products | 1. Ensures the retailer's image as a one-stop shopping experience |
| 2. Is very important to the target customer | 2. Assists in building the image of the retailer as delivering value to the customer | 2. Ensures the image of providing retail value to the target customer | 2. Assists in providing profit margin |
| 3. Leads the other categories in sales, market share, customer satisfaction, and service | 3. Delivers profit and cash flow through sales | 3. Delivers profit and cash flow | |
| 4. Consumes a larger percentage of the retailer's resources such as personnel and technology | 4. Delivers overall growth to the retailer | | |

**FIGURE 6.3** *Summary of Category Roles* (Courtesy of The Partnering Group)

the strategic planning process. Internal factors, such as strong or weak brand names, are classified as strengths and weaknesses, respectively. External factors are classified as opportunities and threats. For example, the emergence of new technology could be either an opportunity or a threat, depending on how the retailer can use the new technology. A SWOT matrix (Figure 6.4) offers four basic strategies:

1. **OS Strategies:** Retailers should pursue these opportunities that play to the strengths of the company.
2. **OW Strategies:** Retailers should overcome the weaknesses before pursuing the opportunities.
3. **TS Strategies:** Retailers should better understand the external threats by fully using its strengths.
4. **TW Strategies:** Retailers should be in a defensive position to avoid external elements from exploiting its weaknesses.

A SWOT analysis is extremely important in assessing the role of the category. The departments and categories within each store unit are important to the overall success of the retailer. Within the store, the impact of the success or failure of one department or category

**FIGURE 6.4** *SWOT Analysis and SWOT Matrix*

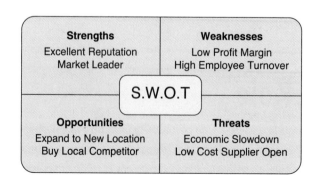

may positively or adversely impact other departments or categories. Therefore, strengths, weaknesses, opportunities, and threats to a category should be determined in order to answer the following questions in regard to the overall strategy of the store, department, and category:

1. How does moving the category to another area of the store impact sales and visibility?
2. How does increasing/decreasing the allocated space impact sales and visibility?
3. How do adding/deleting vendors and/or products impact the customers' impression of the assortment?
4. How do adding/deleting facings of a given product impact category sales and vendor sales?
5. How does moving products to another shelf impact overall category sales and vendor sales?
6. Should we merchandise by brand, retail price, or product type?
7. In planning adjacencies between complementary products, which products should be placed near or in the category?
8. Are the categories defined based on the shopper's behavior and thought process?
9. Are there any cross-merchandising opportunities that I am missing?
10. What other products are bought with this category?
11. Are there any areas in which we are missing opportunities by category, vendor, or product?
12. What products are my competitors selling?
13. What products are sold in other areas of the country by similar retailers?
14. What are the appropriate measures of productivity based on the role the product plays?
15. Which of these questions play to the strengths of the category?
16. Which of these questions threaten the product's ability to serve in a given role?

Once these questions are answered, the retailer can compare the category's SWOT to determine the validity of the assigned role. In summary, the strengths and weaknesses of the category have to be balanced. The threats and opportunities must be assessed. In addition, the retailer must compare the performance of the category with the competition and within the retail chain. The role of a category ultimately impacts the entire retail chain.

# Review

The first step in understanding category management is to begin to understand the role that each product within an assortment or category plays. The customer ultimately decides the role. As a retailer begins to understand the customer, the retailer will begin to understand how to successfully compete for the customer. You begin by creating a baseline of information about the customer, retailer, and market. There are many ways to gather baseline information from both internal and external sources about the market, competition, pertinent financial information, shopper information, and store conditions.

The next step is assigning a role for the category. There are four basic category roles: destination, routine, occasional/seasonal, and convenience. When a category serves as a destination, the customer enters the retailer to buy the products in that category. The second role is the routine category; the customer routinely purchases in this category on a consistent basis.

The third role is the occasional or seasonal category; the customer purchases in this category on a sporadic basis or during certain seasons. The fourth role is the convenience category; these are products that customers purchase infrequently, and are important only when the customer buys them. In order to ensure that the correct role is assigned to a category, an assessment must be implemented. Retailers begin by identifying the strengths, weaknesses, threats, and opportunities (SWOT) of each category.

# key terms

Convenience category   69

Customer relationship management   66

Demographic data   65

Destination category   68

Geo-demographic data   66

Lifestyle data   65

Long Tail   66

Occasional category   68

Pareto's rule   66

Routine category   68

Seasonal category   68

Strengths, weaknesses, threats, and opportunities (SWOT )   69

Supply management   64

Traffic data   65

# activities

- Continued from the activities in Chapter 5, using the category chosen:
  - Describe each retailer's customer.
  - Who are the retailer's direct competitors, including other retail formats?
  - Analyze the store conditions of each, including (1) maintenance, (2) safety and security, (3) parking, (4) store location, (5) desirability of the shopping center, and (6) movement of population in regard to the shopping center (is this a thriving shopping center or a dying shopping center?).
- How does each retailer define the role of the category?
- Prepare a SWOT matrix for the category in each retailer.

# discussion questions

1. What are the four basic category roles in category management?

2. How can products classify as a destination category in one store and as a convenience category in another store?

3. Explain the importance of creating a baseline of information about customers, retailers, and market when determining category roles.

4. Explain the theories of Pareto's role and the Long Tail as it relate to customers and retailing.

# references, resources, web sites, and recommended readings

- Anderson, C. 2008. *The long tail*. New York: Hyperion.
- Food Marketing Institute. http://www.fmi.org/
- Partnering Group. 1995. *Category management report*. Washington, DC: Joint Industry Project on Efficient Consumer Response.

# CATEGORY MANAGEMENT STRATEGIES

7

# Introduction

**Strategy** is the next step in the category management cycle. Before the category strategy is determined, however, the retailer's **vision statement** and **mission statement** must be determined and reviewed. Understanding the relationship between a retailer's vision, overall mission, and resulting strategy is key to creating a plan that may be implemented. Mission can be described as answering the question of "Where are we going?" Strategy is the question of "How do we get there?"

Some retailers also create vision statements that clearly state what the founder of the company envisions for the business. Vision statements are usually broad in scope and often include the founder's idea of the company's value and its contribution to society. Once the vision of the company is established, then strategies, including a mission statement, can be developed.

There are many schools of thought when discussing the mission statement. Most experts agree that a mission statement should be a brief statement focused on the core business of the company and the customers they serve. It should also fit with the vision of the company. A mission statement should answer two simple questions: "What do we do?" and "How do we do it?"

What do we do? This question should be answered in a broader sense than just what the business would normally deliver to a customer. For example, although a retailer offers products to the customer, they are much more than just satisfying the basic needs of their customers. They should consider themselves as providing a great shopping experience to their customers based on price, value, and service.

How do we do it? This question relates to the technical elements of the business. The answer should include the product or service, and how it is delivered to the customers. The product or service should fit the needs of the targeted customer groups. Excellent service and the atmosphere of the retailer all contribute to the customers' overall shopping experience.

Businesses should remember that the vision and mission statements are only guidelines for the business. As the business environment changes, it may be necessary to review these statements and make appropriate changes to stay competitive.

Once the vision and mission statements are developed, businesses will develop strategies to help them achieve their mission and vision. Retailers that use category management as a tool must develop strategies for each category consistent with the retailer's corporate strategy. When assessing the retailer's mission and strategy, several basic questions must be answered:

- What is the image of the retailer? This includes price, assortment, quality, and customer service.
- What are the key performance measures as determined by the retailer and retail analysts? These may include stock turn, GMROII, profit margin, out-of-stock, number of SKUs, rate of returns, customer satisfaction surveys, etc.

# Category Strategies

As shown in Figure 7.1, category strategy is the fifth step in the category management cycle. This is the step where strategies are developed to deliver on the category role and category scorecard. This stage is very important because the strategies also impact the choice of tactics

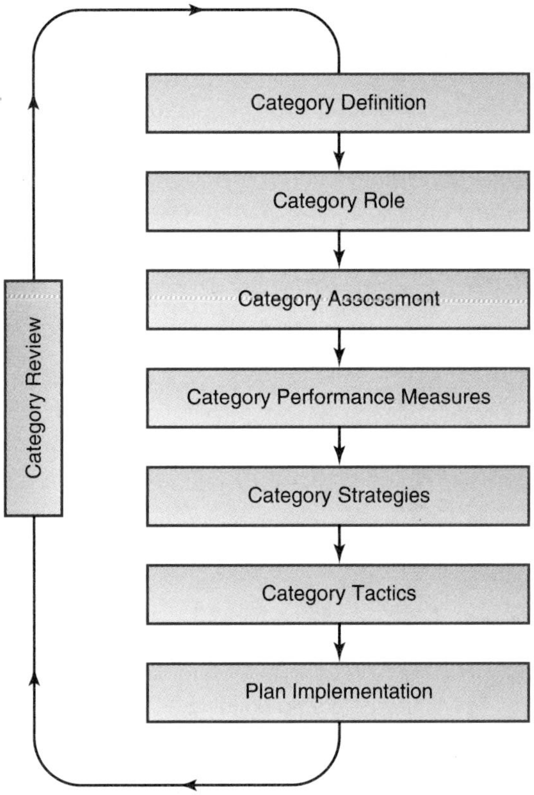

FIGURE 7.1 *Category Management Cycle*
(Courtesy of The Partnering Group)

```
                    ┌──────────────────────────────────┐
                    │                                  │
         ┌──────────┴──────────┐   ┌──────────────────▼──────────────────┐
         │                     │   │        Category Definition           │
         │                     │   └──────────────────┬──────────────────┘
         │                     │                      ▼
         │                     │   ┌──────────────────────────────────────┐
         │                     │   │           Category Role               │
         │                     │   └──────────────────┬──────────────────┘
         │                     │                      ▼
         │   Category Review   │   ┌──────────────────────────────────────┐
         │                     │   │        Category Assessment            │
         │                     │   └──────────────────┬──────────────────┘
         │                     │                      ▼
         │                     │   ┌──────────────────────────────────────┐
         │                     │   │   Category Performance Measures       │
         │                     │   └──────────────────┬──────────────────┘
         │                     │                      ▼
         │                     │   ┌──────────────────────────────────────┐
         │                     │   │         Category Strategies           │
         │                     │   └──────────────────┬──────────────────┘
         │                     │                      ▼
         │                     │   ┌──────────────────────────────────────┐
         │                     │   │          Category Tactics             │
         │                     │   └──────────────────┬──────────────────┘
         │                     │                      ▼
         │                     │   ┌──────────────────────────────────────┐
         └──────────┬──────────┘   │        Plan Implementation            │
                    │              └──────────────────┬──────────────────┘
                    └─────────────────────────────────┘
```

in developing the category. Tactics are discussed in the next chapter. The development of category strategies has five basic drivers:

1. Total number of shopping trips
2. Percentage of shopping trips that contain the category
3. Value transaction of the market basket
4. Gross margin
5. Actual profit

Each of these drivers can be assessed by reviewing the customer's market basket. Retailers assess the number of shopping trips by analyzing POS data and associating the data with a credit card or loyalty card. They try to determine why a customer makes multiple trips to a store, and identify the product that necessitates the trip. For instance, a motivator of grocery shopping is often perishable goods such as dairy, meat, vegetables, and bread. Once the data are analyzed, retailers can make judgments about the appropriate strategy for each product and the role the product plays. In addition to purchase frequency, retailers also review the actual value of the market basket by determining the total amount spent, as well as the gross margin of each item and the profitability of the total basket. Retailers assign strategies and roles to categories and products. They also decide which products/categories should be placed near other categories/products.

Retailers and vendors assess several criteria when choosing the appropriate strategy. The category management team seeks to focus on growth and profit by:

1. Increasing the number of shoppers or traffic
2. Increasing the transaction size and/or transaction profit
3. Creating excitement
4. Enhancing the image of the retailer
5. Defending the retailer's target market and historical customer base

*Market Basket - numbers of items in the basket*

| Strategies | Purpose |
|---|---|
| Traffic Building | Draw customers into the store |
| Transaction Building | Increase register amount; higher sales for each ticket |
| Excitement Creation | Build shoppers' excitement |
| Image Enhancing | Reinforce retailer image of variety, quality, price, service, etc. |
| Turf Protecting | Defend market share |

**FIGURE 7.2** *Category Strategies* (Courtesy of The Partnering Group)

The category management team must determine the correct strategy for each category. Figure 7.2 shows the five strategies that are often used to increase the effectiveness of categories. Each strategy plays a significant role in the success of the category; the first two build sales and profitability, the third and fourth focus on how the customer perceives the retailer, and the fifth emphasizes maintaining customer loyalty.

# Traffic Building

The first strategy is **traffic building**, which focuses on bringing customers into a store, aisle, or category. These are frequently purchased products that serve as a **destination category**. Retailers depend on traffic-building categories and products to increase overall sales and profitability. For instance, soft drinks serve as traffic builders when retailers offer them at a lower-than-normal price. When a retailer offers four packages for the same price as they usually offer for two packages, they will likely generate greater traffic into the store. These on-sale products are often classified as "loss leaders." They do not generate profit themselves, but attract customers into the store because of the sale, and hopefully lead them to purchase other items or products from the store. Products serving other roles may serve as traffic-building categories, including routine, or occasional/seasonal. This strategy is important because once in the store, customers may purchase other products that fall within other retail strategies, such as transaction building.

# Transaction Building

The second strategy is **transaction building**, which focuses on increasing the size of the category, aisle, or store transaction. These are products that, by their nature, encourage the customer to purchase other products, thus building the transaction. Transaction building products may serve in the role of destination, routine, occasional/seasonal, or convenience. An example of a product serving in the **destination role** is premium deli meat like Boar's Head. When a product serves the destination role, the mission of the customer is to purchase that particular product. For instance, many customers seek grocery stores selling this brand of deli meat, but rarely purchase deli meat alone. They also likely purchase bread, cheese, condiments, pickles, and chips. Customers may also buy other items on their grocery list simply because of the convenience of a making a single stop. An example of a product serving in the **routine role** is cat food. Cat owners frequently purchase cat food; however, the mission of the shopping experience may not be to purchase cat food. The customer purchasing cat food is also likely to build the transaction by also purchasing cat litter or cat toys. An example of a product serving in the **occasional/seasonal role** is Halloween candy. A customer rarely buys just one package of Halloween candy. They also likely purchase Halloween decorative items, decorated cookies, and Halloween costumes. An example of a product serving in the **convenience role** is candles. When a customer seeks tea light candles for a special event, while in the candle area they are much more likely to purchase other candles they may need in the future, new votives, and maybe matches or a lighter. Impulse items such as magazines and candy placed at the checkout areas are transaction-building products that also serve in the **convenience role**.

Products serving in the strategy of **transaction building** are vital to the success of a retailer. Most apparel chain retailers expect at least three items on a ticket. They encourage their sales associates to promote add-on sales; examples include a belt with jeans, jewelry with tops, or socks with shoes. Sales associates are often trained to encourage add-on sales or to build the transaction. For example, Chico's places the mirrors outside the dressing rooms to ensure the customer and sales associates have an opportunity to interact, thereby increasing the likelihood of an add-on sale.

# Excitement Creation

**Excitement creation** is the third strategy often used to ensure success in category management. Excitement-creation products are often impulse items, seasonal, or lifestyle oriented. Department stores use this strategy when they bring in a new and popular brand. These brands are usually higher-end brands with a national, yet narrow, following. Specialty stores usually focus on seasonal products, and grocery stores on impulse items. Williams-Sonoma and Pottery Barn are excellent examples of retailers that successfully market to the lifestyle customer through three major channels: retail stores, catalogs, and the Internet. Williams-Sonoma offers personalized items, food products, and dinnerware for all occasions. Pottery Barn focuses on high-quality, comfortable, and stylish furniture and household goods. Zara and H&M are apparel retailers that create an exciting retail environment. Both retailers are classified as fast fashion retailers with minimal inventories and the reputation for not replenishing products. If you see something you like in either retailer, you know you must buy it when you see it. This feeling of immediacy creates excitement in the store.

# Image Enhancing

The fourth strategy is **image enhancing**. This strategy focuses on frequently purchased, highly promoted, unique, or seasonal items. These products and categories focus on ensuring the retailer's image in any of the following areas: price, service, quality, and assortment. Because this strategy covers so many areas, the method by which a retailer uses this strategy depends on the retailer type. Wal-Mart focuses on price, Nordstrom on customer service, and Crane & Company on high-quality stationery. This strategy is most closely related to the vision and mission of the retailer. Rather than the retailer focusing on price, assortment, quality, or customer service, this strategy focuses on ensuring that the customer understands who the retailer is.

# Turf Defending

The fifth strategy is **turf defending**, used by retailers to maintain their traditional customer base and defend their position with the competition. PetSmart uses dog and cat food as turf-defending products. They rely on offering an overwhelming assortment of pet food that discourages most mass merchandisers or grocery stores from competing with them head-on. Another example of turf defending is how Target uses trendy apparel and trendy house-wares to defend their territory. This strategy is closely aligned with the excitement-creating and image-enhancing strategies. The big difference is that this strategy ensures that the retailer's vision and mission are implemented by comparing the retailer with the competitors. This is a defensive strategy; the excitement-creating and image-enhancing strategies are designed to build a positive relationship with the customer rather than making a comparison with another retailer.

All of these strategies were developed to ensure the successful implementation of category management. They focus on generating cash flow and increasing the retailer's profit contribution. Each should be assessed continually in the category management cycle. However, retailing is changing. The newest strategy impacting all aspects of the retailing culture, including category management, is **sustainability**. However, the impact of sustainability is broader than the product, and the role the product plays in the retailer. The next section discusses sustainability as a cultural change within retailing. The impact of each initiative will be seen far into the future and ultimately change retailing.

# Sustainability as a Retail Strategy

Category management began as an initiative of Efficient Consumer Response; the newest efficiency movement is sustainability. Retailers focus on becoming good corporate citizens in regard to the environment. The major purposes of sustainability are to: (1) reduce **carbon emissions** by lowering the usage of pollution-producing fuels, or changing to fuels like solar energy or wind power that do not produce carbon dioxide emissions; and (2) reduce or eliminate the amount of refuse by recycling.

The Retail Industry Leaders Association (RILA) began to push socially sustainable objectives and business practices in 2007. At that time, the two major areas were (1) environmentally friendly landscaping, and (2) improving the supply chain to reduce emissions. In 2009, Global Retail Insights noted that sustainability is increasing in importance to retailers' survival throughout the world. There are core business practices that lead to the development of a retailer's sustainability strategy, including costs, customers, and competitors, in addition to government regulations. The United Kingdom enacted the Climate Change Bill, which forces companies to cut carbon emissions by 60% by 2050. The question for companies is not whether their governments will enact requirements to lower carbon emissions, but when they will enact them.

The Food Marketing Institute has identified areas in which retailers are establishing green initiatives. Their first is to reduce waste by:

1. Recycling
2. Reusable bags
3. Reduce retailers' own packaging
4. Collaboration with supply chain partners to eliminate or reduce packaging
5. Participating in collaborative efforts with government groups

The institute also addresses the issue of carbon emissions, or the amount of carbon dioxide produced by the production, transportation, or selling of retail products. They proposed that retailers can reduce carbon emissions by:

1. Energy-efficient lighting systems, including high-efficiency fluorescents, LED lighting, daylight, motion sensors, and solar-powered skylights
2. Improvement of refrigeration efficiency and maintenance
3. New store design technology, including evaporative cooling and radiant heat flooring
4. Upgrading transportations systems

Energy and materials' intensive supply chains, such as the transportation of products, account for approximately 75% of a company's carbon emissions. By accurately anticipating customer demands, retailers can make more efficient purchases based on actual need, and transport only those goods needed the shortest distance possible with a full truck load. The ultimate goal is to eliminate overpurchasing, overproduction, and ultimately waste. Each retailer takes a different approach to sustainability; however, each initiative will probably become part of the retail culture as the movement progresses.

Walmart began an aggressive program to implement green initiatives within their own companies and with their vendors. The three areas they focus on are: (1) energy climate, (2) waste, and (3) products. Walmart's Web site has a link to the sustainability initiatives, which includes their goal of "to be supplied 100% by renewable energy; to create zero waste; and to sell products that sustain our resources and environment." Target hopes to eliminate PVC from their store-branded products. Staples was the first retailer to reward customers for recycling any brand of ink or toner cartridges. In addition to recycling, they focus on three other areas for operating as a more sustainable company—offering environmentally preferable products, energy conservation and renewable energy, and environmental education. JCPenney developed a new store prototype that includes bricks made from recycled products, local sourcing of materials, low-wattage LED lights, and occupancy sensors in offices, restrooms, dressing rooms, and stockrooms. Whole Foods developed a 3 R's program: reduce, reuse, and recycle. They are implementing paperless ordering systems, composting, and banning plastic grocery bags. They are also developing a solar energy program, as well as constructing buildings using green building techniques. Wegmans implemented a seafood plan whereby they will not sell any seafood species that has a sustainability concern. Home Depot added the EcoOptions Web site that includes information on sustainable forestry, clean air, a healthy home, water conservation, energy efficiency, and a virtual tour of the EcoOptions home.

Sustainability is becoming embedded in retailers' strategies and tactics. Like with the implementation of any new strategy, including category management, a sustainability initiative must be adopted by the retailer's top management. As retailers see a positive impact in operating costs and the environment in areas like energy management, recycling, transportation, construction, and supplier packaging reduction, reluctant retailers will join the sustainability movement.

# Review

Strategy is the next step in the category management cycle; however, before determining the category strategy, the retailer's vision and mission must be determined and reviewed. Once these are developed, businesses develop strategies to help them achieve their vision and mission. This step is where strategies are developed to deliver on the category role and category scorecard. This stage is very important because the strategies also impact the choice of tactics in developing the category.

Each strategy plays a significant role in the success of the category; the first two build sales and profitability, the third and fourth focus on how the customer perceives the retailer, and the fifth emphasize maintaining customer loyalty. The five strategies used to increase the effectiveness of categories are: (1) traffic building, (2) transaction building, (3) excitement creation, (4) image enhancing, and (5) turf defending. Traffic building focuses on bringing customers into a store, aisle, or category. Transaction building focuses on increasing the size of the category, aisle, or store transaction. Excitement creation is often used to ensure success in category management by offering impulse, seasonal, or lifestyle-oriented items that the customer finds compelling. The image-enhancing strategy focuses on frequently purchased, highly promoted, unique, or seasonal items that ensures the retailer's image in any of the following areas: price, service, quality, and assortment. Turf defending is used by retailers to maintain their traditional customer base and defend their position with the competition. All these strategies were developed to ensure the successful implementation of category management. They focus on generating cash flow and increasing the retailer's profit contribution. Each should be assessed continually in the category management cycle. However, retailing is changing and the newest strategy impacting all aspects of the retailing culture, including category management, is sustainability. Sustainability is becoming embedded in the strategies and tactics of retailers. As retailers see a positive impact in operating costs and the environment in areas like energy management, recycling, transportation, construction, and supplier packaging reduction, reluctant retailers will join the sustainability movement.

# key terms

# activities

- From the category chosen in Chapter 5:
  - Give examples of products in each store serving in each strategy.
- Choose five categories commonly found in three types of retailers. Explain how the categories of merchandise can serve different strategies based on the type of retailer.
- Review the annual reports of 10 retailers. Summarize their efforts in creating a sustainable retail environment.

# discussion questions

1. Explain how a vision statement leads to the development of the mission statement and overall retail strategy.

2. How is the image of a retailer related to the mission statement?

3. What are typical measures of productivity used by retailers that focus on each of the following: price, assortment, quality, and customer service?

4. List the drivers of category management strategies, and relate each to a strategy.

5. List the five basic strategies, and give examples of each.

6. How does the role of a product or category impact the strategy?

7. Why is sustainability important to retailers?

8. How are retailers becoming sustainable?

9. Give examples of how sustainability impacts the five basic strategies of category management.

# references, resources, web sites, and recommended Readings

- Home Depot. http://www.homedepot.com/
- Staples. http://staples.com/
- Target. http://target.com/
- Walmart. http://walmart.com/
- Wegmans. http://wegmans.com/

# CATEGORY

# TACTICS

**LEARNING GOALS**

On completion of this chapter, the student will be able to:

- List the five tactics of category management.
- Explain the four major assessment areas of the assortment tactic.
- List the four choices that retailers make in regard to the assortment tactic.
- Discuss the four choices that retailers make in regard to the pricing tactic.
- Explain product clustering.
- Explain the concept of price elasticity.
- List the benchmarks of the pricing strategy.
- Give examples of the decisions related to promotions.
- Explain how the merchandising strategy impacts the core values of retailing.
- List the attributes that impact the implementation of the merchandising tactic.
- Explain how retailers micro-market or type their stores.

8

# Introduction

After retailers define the category, they begin to understand the role that each product within an assortment or category plays. The next step is choosing the appropriate strategy. Once the role and strategy for a category are determined, the next step is to develop the tactics to achieve the goals and objectives set for the category, and then finally implement these steps. Tactics enable retailers to focus on each action necessary to successfully implement category management. This chapter discusses the five basic tactics of category management, and gives examples of how retailers use these tactics.

# Category Tactics

The goal of **category tactics** is to choose a specific action to achieve a specific strategy based on the role the category plays. In determining the appropriate tactic, retailers review the four basic category roles: destination, routine, occasional/seasonal, and convenience. These roles determine how the retailer makes decisions about the implementation of each tactic. The five areas of tactics are: (1) assortment, (2) pricing, (3) promotion, (4) merchandising, and (5) micro-marketing. Figure 8.1 shows the five category tactics. This process must include all personnel, including category management, store operations, merchandising, and regional directors/store managers. Each is important in determining the appropriate tactic for success. Store operations personnel must determine the impact and timing of the store rollout of new products. They also assist the category management team with timing new product introductions, **delists**, promotional calendars, and merchandising recommendations. A **delist** is a list of products eliminated from the assortment. The merchandising team helps determine the appropriate timing for a change in merchandising. The regional directors and store managers are critical to the success of any program; if the retailer wants to make any changes, their buy-in to the change is crucial.

**FIGURE 8.1** *Category Tactics* (Courtesy of The Partnering Group)

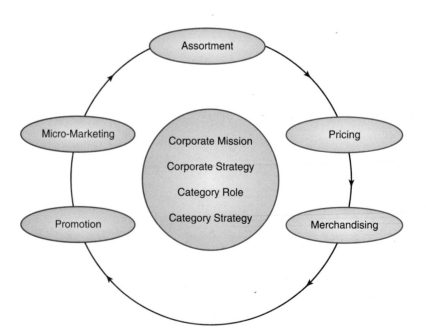

# Assortment Tactic

The first tactic is determining the optimal assortment for the retailer. The category management team may decide to (1) maintain the assortment, (2) eliminate or delist products from the assortment, or (3) add new products to the assortment. Although the assortment is determined by the category management team and the retailer, the assortment must focus on the consumers' perception of the number and variety of items offered in an assortment. In addition, the assortment is assessed to determine which brands and segments within the category are driving category growth. The category sales and sales performance of new products are assessed to determine the viability of the product.

The first decision in determining the optimal assortment that a category management team makes is in regard to their **breadth** or **depth of assortment**. Breadth of an assortment is the number of brands carried in a category. Depth of an assortment is the number of stockkeeping units within each brand in a category. For instance, soup is common category in grocery stores. The breadth of the assortment includes the number of different soups by composition, size, and brand. An example of depth and breadth is the linear feet used to display soups. The breadth of the assortment is the number of brands of soups offered by a grocery store, such as Campbell's, Progresso, and a store's private label brand. The depth includes the number of facings and the number of containers behind the facing(s). A facing is the number of units on the front of a shelf facing the customer. **Assortment tactics** enable retailers to make four crucial decisions: (1) maintain the assortment, (2) decrease the assortment, (3) increase the assortment, or (4) change the assortment.

Choosing the best assortment depends on a number of variables: (1) the wants, needs, and previous behavior of the target customer; (2) changes in the vendors' offerings; (3) trends in the area; (4) overall marketing strategy; (5) cost versus benefit of changing the assortment; and (6) criteria for deleting products. The category management team must research the market to determine if their assortment has any missing SKUs, and whether any of the products in the current assortment are unproductive. Two key determinants of productivity are turnover and sales. However, the team must also assess the product's role as ensuring the retailer's strategy. For instance, using the example of soups again, chicken noodle soup may have a lower turnover than other soups, but the customer expects chicken noodle soup to be available within the assortment, thus meeting the strategy of convenience.

When analyzing the assortment, four major areas are assessed: (1) customer behavior and loyalty, (2) productivity indicators, (3) category status, and (4) market trends and comparison. The category management team needs to determine how a customer shops the category, and what products or brands within the category the customer considers to be essential, based on their loyalty patterns and product substitution patterns. There are many productivity indicators, including: sales, profit, turnover, Gross Margin Return on Inventory Investment (GMROII), **return on assets (ROA)**, and sales per cubic, linear, and/or square feet. Gross Margin Return on Inventory Investment is the relationship between gross margin and stock turn. This category status includes both new product introductions and product deletions by brand or category. Retailers and vendors must be aware of trends in the market, including the variety offered by the retailer, retail channel, and competition (Partnering Group 1995 and ECR Europe 2000). If the retailer decides to maintain the assortment as is, the retailer will continue to monitor the category.

The second choice is to decrease the category by reducing the number of SKUs in a category, subcategory, or segment. Before a SKU is deleted or delisted, the sales and productivity data must be carefully analyzed to determine whether the product contributes to either the overall financial performance of the category or the satisfaction level of the customer. Retailers need to review a number of criteria when deciding whether to delete a product or minimize the space allocation:

1. Is the product duplicated in the category? If the product is duplicated and the customer is likely to switch brands, delisting is a possibility.
2. Are customers loyal to the product? If the customers are loyal, retailers may need to keep the product and reassign a strategy to this product.
3. Is the product costing valuable space and reducing overall turnover in the category? If the product is lowering turnover and a more productive product needs more space, the product probably needs to be delisted.
4. Is the product important in maintaining the image of the category? Some products are not as productive as others, but provide the image associated with the retailer's strategy. If this is the case, the retailer will keep the product, but may limit the number of facings.
5. Are the sales of the product growing over time? When sales continue to increase, the overall space allocation may change to include more facings.
6. Are there new products in this market? New products change the dynamics of a category. For instance, when low-carbohydrate diets were popular, many new products were introduced but then deleted when the fad faded.
7. How will new products impact the assortment? New products added to an assortment in the same amount of space limit the number of facings for other products or force other products to be delisted.

The third choice is whether to add a new product to a category. When introducing a new product, the decision is not as simple as just deciding whether to add something new to the merchandising mix, but involves a complete analysis of the entire supply chain. Some pertinent questions to ask are:

- What changes are needed to the shelf space? Retailers must determine how much space is needed to adequately stock and merchandise the new product.
- How easy is the product to merchandise? The type and size of the product and/or the container impact the retailer's ability to merchandise the product. A loose product, such as nuts and bolts, must be in a container on the shelf, other items need to be hung from a pegboard, and very large items need to be placed on a lower shelf. All of these factors impact the ability of the retailer to merchandise the product.
- What are the **handling costs** of adding a new product? The number of times that employees handle a product increases the cost of adding a new product. Many grocery stores handle loose fruits and vegetables a number of times, thus increasing the cost.
- How will the distribution center handle the product? The number of steps necessary for a distribution center to handle a product impacts the desirability of the retailer stocking the product. For instance, (1) steps that are automated are more desirable than those that are manual, (2) products that use cross-docking are more desirable than those housed for a

time in a distribution center, and (3) having a product delivered directly to the store increases the product's desirability (ECR Europe 2000).

Planning the assortment is extremely important to the success of the retailer. Whether the retailer is changing the assortment by adding or deleting products, or changing the space allocation, the category management team must carefully analyze all of the factors discussed above.

# Pricing Tactic

Determining the optimal **pricing** structure is crucial to a retailer's success and involves an analysis of both marketing and financial data. Categories, and products within categories, are assessed by price point and their contribution to both the category and retailer's image and profitability objectives. Several factors must be considered when determining the **price point** for a product:

1. Expected profit margin
2. Retail strategy
3. Any dynamics in the category regarding pricing

The **price point** is the range of prices offered by a retail store. Different types of retailers have different pricing issues based on their retail strategy and image. Grocery stores and mass merchandisers usually choose between everyday low prices or high—low pricing strategies. Possible pricing choices are:

1. Maintain the current pricing
2. Decrease the prices of all or part of a category
3. Increase the prices of all or part of the category
4. Cluster the prices by product characteristics within a category

Retailers analyze the current pricing based on past history and by comparing their pricing structure to that of their competitors. If they find that their prices are not competitive, they may increase or decrease the prices of all or part of the merchandise within a category. Their other choice is to cluster their prices based on product characteristics. For instance, low-fat or low carbohydrate cookies may be priced differently than other types of cookies because their desirability may be greater to the consumer.

The first step in brand **clustering** products is determining the market position of the brands within the category. Within a category you have premium brands, the market leader; the secondary product or brand; and tertiary products or brands, each positioned in the market differently. Pricing based on marketing position is common in all aspects of retailing: automotive, apparel, grocery, or furniture. The second step is to group products by **elasticity**. Elasticity is stability in pricing terms; it is determined by a qualitative assessment by the category manager based on experience. There are three categories of elasticity: super dynamics (category is checked daily or twice a week), dynamic (price is checked weekly or every two weeks), or static (price is checked monthly or every three months).

Retailers must also determine how the product contributes to margin goals and where there are opportunities in regard to the competitor's prices. The category management team assesses the competition, the **price elasticity**, and finally reviews sales, gross margin, and contribution to the welfare of the category. The final benchmarks to determine the success of the pricing strategy are:

1. **Penetration and traffic**—Products purchased frequently by the target customer.
2. **Conversion**—Products used to entice or convert customers to shop a new category.
3. **Spending and transaction size**—Products purchased by big spenders who spend more money than others and have a large market basket indicating a large number of items.
4. **Loyalty and frequency**—Products purchased by loyal customers that need to always be in stock.

When products build a price image, and the price is set at the right price to build traffic, this is known as penetration and traffic. Conversion is using price to convert a shopper to a buyer. The spending and transaction size is assessed by the POS data. To ensure loyalty and frequency of purchase, retailers need to set the price to maintain loyal customers and encourage them to purchase frequently. To ensure that customers remain loyal, you also need to determine how customers react to price. If they are extremely price sensitive, there is very little flexibility in setting the retail price. You must also determine the pricing relationship between segments within the category. For instance, in the category of baking products, cake mix and frosting are usually placed in adjacent shelves. If the customer perceives the cake mix is priced too high, the customer will forgo the purchase of both the cake mix and the icing. If the customer perceives the price as too low, the volume of sales may increase because the customer participates in forward buying. The customer also shops at other retailers; therefore, they can determine whether the pricing structure is competitive. Pricing is a complicated, yet important, tactic in retailing.

# Promotion Tactic

The category management team must determine the optimal promotional strategies for a product, category, and the retailer based on the category roles of destination, routine, occasional/seasonal, or convenience. Several decisions relate to promotions:

1. Choosing the type of promotion
2. Choosing the product(s) to be promoted
3. Determining the intensity of promotions including the timing and frequency
4. Assessing the effectiveness of the promotion by volume sold and profit generation
5. Cross-merchandising and tie-in promotions
6. Comparing your promotions to your competitors

Many types of promotions are used in retailing, such as Super Bowl promotions, point of purchase displays (POP), coupons, frequent buyer incentives, product demonstrations and sampling, fashion shows, themed promotions such as Fourth of July promotions, newspaper advertisements, and signage. Data from past promotions are often analyzed to determine the success and/or failure of a particular format of promotion. Several factors must be considered when choosing products to promote, including brand loyalty, current sales of the product, stage within the lifespan of the product, and competitor's promotional strategy. Some products are promoted with more intensity than others; sometimes you see a combination of several types of promotion, such as television advertisements, point of purchase displays, and coupons. Customers begin to anticipate the timing of promotions, based on previous experience with retailers. Black Friday (the day after Thanksgiving), December 26th, white sales in February, and school supply sales are all anticipated promotions during the year.

Timing is also important when a new product is introduced or when sales are not meeting projections. The promotional calendar maintained by a retailer or vendor is usually planned in advance so that activities can be coordinated. The frequency of promotions depends on a number of factors, including past history, current sales, planned product introductions, and end-of-season sales. Retailers and vendors are interested in the volume sold on promotion. This is the number of products sold at the promotional price. Finally, cross-merchandising opportunities and tie-in promotions are evident throughout the year. For instance, during Cinco de Mayo, retailers promote beer, margarita mix, chips, salsa, guacamole dip, and Latino music.

Promotion is an important tactic in retailing; however, promotion can be expensive unless the retailer and vendors carefully evaluate the success of the promotions as judged by sales, gross margin, or new customer trials. Promotion is a changing tactic with technology both in the home and in the retailer. **Digital Video Recorders (DVRs)** are lowering the effectiveness of television commercials because customers can now fast forward through the commercials on recorded programs. **Product placement** is thus becoming more important. Product placement is becoming more common in television and movies. When you see an actor holding a can of soft drink with the logo clearly facing the audience, you can assume the vendor paid for the product to be held in that manner during the taping of the television program or movie.

# Merchandising Tactic

This tactic focuses on the core values of retailing and marketing: the right product in the right place in the right quantities at the right time. The core question is "has the retailer planned the space well?" The **merchandising tactic** focuses on the optimal use of space, signage, and adjacencies for the retailer. Category management teams use software programs such as JDA Intactix Space Planning, IRI's Apollo, or ACNielsen's Spaceman to optimize space allocation. These software products assist the category management team manage space, analyze data, implement planograms, and place new products. When implementing the merchandising tactic, you must assess the following attributes:

1. **Category location in the store and the aisle:** Destination merchandise is traditionally placed around the perimeter of the store. Category management includes an additional destination area: the center of the aisle. If a customer walks to the center of an aisle, they are more likely to walk the length of the aisle, thereby walking by and hopefully purchasing other items in addition to their intended purchase.

2. **Shelf layout within the category:** The best to place to put merchandise with the highest mark-up or greatest profitability is on shelves located between an adult's elbow and eye. For children, the best location is shopping cart height. Think of cereals: adult cereals are placed at adult sight level; children's cereals are placed on lower shelves.

3. **Minimum Days of Supply:** the minimum days of supply before the next delivery. The term min–max is often used to indicate both the minimum and maximum number of units

of a given product that will optimally meet the needs of the customer. Retailers seek to minimize or eliminate an out-of-stock situation by determining the min–max.

4. **Shelf capacity** or **packout:** the number of units within a single SKU on a shelf.
5. **Segments and subsegments within the category:** all variations within the segment identified by the customer decision-making tree and vendors.
6. **Space allocation:** the amount of space allocated to a category within a store.
7. **Signage and promotions within the category** (Partnering Group 1995).

You must also ensure that the merchandising suits the target customer, allows each vendor to be differentiated, and that the merchandising is consistent with the category role and strategies. Upon completing the assessment, a planogram is developed. If a planogram is successful, customers will be drawn to the category and the adjacencies, and there will be enough stock to ensure there are no out of stocks (OOS).

The merchandising tactic is the visible portrayal of category management. When customers shop in any retailer using category management, the success or failure of the merchandising tactic becomes obvious. Customers seeking a specific product may not find the product for any number of reasons—it may be in stock or out of stock based on the projected demand and the on-time delivery and stocking of the product. A common challenge for shoppers is determining the correct aisle for a product. Some products are seemingly obvious, whereas others may be ambiguous. For instance, most grocery stores and mass merchandisers include pecans and walnuts in the baking aisle, whereas others place nuts in the snack aisle. A customer planning to bake a pecan pie or walnut brownies assumes pecans and walnuts will be included in the baking aisle; instead, the walnuts and pecans have been defined by the retailer as a snack and are placed in the snack aisle. The customer becomes frustrated and may forgo the purchase. This illustrates one of the challenges in merchandising. The snack aisle includes peanuts and popcorn; walnuts and pecans are nuts, but not necessarily snacking nuts. In a situation like this you have to focus on the customer's thought process rather than that of the vendor or the type of product.

A merchandising checklist was developed and presented in the ECR Report "How to implement Consumer Enthusiasm—Strategic Consumer Value Management." Here is an adaptation:

1. Is the merchandising in line with the strategic position and objectives while focusing on the target customer?
2. Does the merchandising meet the needs of the target customer?
3. Does the merchandising reflect the category definition, strategy, and role?
4. Is there a clear overview of the assortment of choices available?
5. Does the merchandising set reflect the customer decision-making tree?
6. Are categories located "logically" to the customer in order to drive sales?
7. Are related categories located near one another?
8. Does the placement of the category within the store encourage impulse purchases as well as planned purchases?
9. Is the merchandising conducive to add-one purchases?
10. Is the signage correct?
11. Does the merchandising fit the overall strategy and mission of the store?
12. Does the merchandising create the desired environment to attract and keep the target customer? (ECR Europe 2000).

# Micro-marketing

The final, or maybe the first, tactic is **micro-marketing**, depending on your perspective. In order for the other tactics to succeed, you must know who your primary customer is while realizing that no single type of customer shops a category. Typical information retailers seek about customers in order to type or micro-market to them are:

1. Who shops the category by demographic and lifestyle factors including age, race, gender, income, lifestyle, and life stage?
2. Among a single group that is typed, do they all buy the same or similar products?
3. How often do they shop?
4. How much do they spend?
5. What merchandise does their market basket contain?
6. Do they buy in the same quantity as other shoppers?
7. How do they make their buying decisions?
8. Are they our core customer?
9. How do they compare to other shoppers in other areas of the country?

When planning the micro-marketing for a category, retailers must consider how consumer demographics and lifestyle affects their buying behavior. When there are variations in the customer segments, they have to decide on the best approach to micro-market to the target customer without alienating other customers. Retailers often **cluster** stores based on the similarities of customers determined by demographics, lifestyles, and buying behavior. For instance, retailers may classify stores by race, income, lifestage, weather, family size, religious preferences, or region of the country. A store micro-marketing to young families carries different merchandise than a store targeting older adults. Although the stores may be close in distance to one another, the core or target customer is different and influences the merchandise assortment.

Each category is assigned a strategy based on the role the category plays for the retailer. The tactics enable retailers to effectively pursue their strategies based on the data provided in that category. Although they may become routine after a time, a careful and thorough reassessment benefits both retailers and their vendors.

# Review

The goal of category tactics is to choose a specific action to achieve a specific strategy. The five tactic areas are: (1) assortment, (2) pricing, (3) promotion, (4) merchandising, and (5) micro-marketing. The first tactic is to determine the optimal assortment for the retailer. The category management team decides whether to (1) maintain the assortment, (2) eliminate certain products, or (3) add new products. The assortment has four major areas of assessment: (1) customer behavior and loyalty, (2) productivity indicators, (3) category status, and (4) market trends and comparison.

Determining the optimal pricing structure is crucial to a retailer's success, and involves an analysis of both marketing and financial data. Categories, and products within categories, are assessed by price point and their contribution to the category and the retailer's image and profitability objectives. When determining the **price point** of a product, you must consider:

(1) the wholesale price of the product, (2) the expected profit margin, (3) the retail strategy, and (4) any dynamics in the category regarding pricing.

The category management team must determine the optimal promotional strategies for a product, category, and the retailer. Many types of promotions are used in retailing, such as Super Bowl promotions, **point of purchase displays (POP)**, coupons, frequent buyer incentives, product demonstrations and sampling, fashion shows, themed promotions such as Fourth of July promotions, newspaper advertisements, and signage. Several decisions relate to promotions: (1) choosing the type of promotion; (2) choosing the product(s) to be promoted; (3) determining the intensity of promotions, including the timing and frequency; (4) assessing the effectiveness by volume sold and profit generation of the promotion; (5) cross-merchandising and tie-in promotions (Partnering Group 1995); and (6) comparing your promotions to your competitors (ECR Europe 2000).

This tactic focuses on the core values of retailing and marketing: the right product in the right place in the right quantities at the right time. The core question is, "Has the retailer planned the space well?" The merchandising tactic focuses on the optimal use of space, signage, and adjacencies. It is the visible portrayal of category management. When customers shop in any retailer using category management, the success or failure of the merchandising tactic becomes obvious.

The final, or maybe first, tactic is micro-marketing, depending on your perspective. In order for the other tactics to succeed, you must know your primary customer while realizing that no single type of customer shops a category. When planning the micro-marketing for a category, you must consider how consumer demographics and lifestyle affect their buying behavior. When there are variations in the customer segments, you have to decide on the best approach to micro-market to the target customer without alienating other customers.

# key terms

Assortment tactic   87

Breadth of assortment   87

Category tactics   86

Clustering   89

Delist   86

Depth of assortment   87

Digital Video Recorder (DVR)   91

Handling costs   88

Merchandising tactic   91

Micro-marketing   93

Minimum Days of Supply   91

Packout   92

Point of purchase display (POP)   94

Price elasticity   90

Price point   89

Pricing tactic   89

Product placement   91

Promotion tactic   90

Return on assets   87

Shelf capacity   92

# activities

- Give examples of retailers you think exemplify each of the tactics.
- Explain how a change in tactics affects the category.
- Visit a grocery store or mass merchandiser and complete the survey by watching 10 consumers shop an aisle. Record the:

- Length of time in the aisle
- Number of products purchased
- Level of shelf from which the product was purchased (knee, waist, eye, above eye level).

## discussion questions

1. List and define the five tactics of category management.
2. Discern between breadth and depth of assortment.
3. List the four choices involved in assortment planning.
4. Give examples of products with different levels of elasticity.
5. List and define the benchmarks related to pricing strategy.
6. What is the advantage for retailers to cluster stores?

## references, resources, web sites, and recommended readings

- ECR Europe. 2000. *The essential guide to day to day category management.*

- Partnering Group. 1995. *Category management report.* Washington, DC: Joint Industry Project on Efficient Consumer Response.

# SHOPPER INSIGHTS

**LEARNING GOALS**

On completion of this chapter, the student will be able to:

- Explain how the concept of shopper insights changed retailing.
- List the facets of the retail experience.
- Cite the modes of communication between the retailer and shopper.
- Explain the three activation points of retailers and shoppers.
- Identify the myths of retailing with the reality of shopper behavior.
- Differentiate the internal drivers of shopping behavior and the in-store drivers of shopping behavior.
- Summarize the data collection techniques that retailers use.
- Differentiate between the shopper segmentation strategies.
- Compare the four different modes of shopping.
- Compare the new category management cycle with the old cycle.
- Evaluate the benefits of including shopper insights.
- Draw the new category management cycle.

# Introduction

Retailing is constantly changing, including the way retailers implement category management. In the recent past, retailers were so focused on implementing the technological applications discussed in previous chapters that they often lost sight of the shopping experience. They thought there was a tradeoff: efficiency versus a focus on customer experience. The newest evolution of category management is the inclusion of **shopper insights**. This chapter focuses on shopper insights and the new category management cycle developed by the Partnering Group in 2009 for the Food Marketing Institute.

Customers have choices in the retail landscape. They can choose the retailer, the time they shop, and the products and quantities they buy. Customers have opinions about every facet of the retail experience, including: the (1) store's physical environment and location, (2) employee's knowledge level and attitudes, (3) quality and quantity of the store's product assortment, (4) store's commitment to the environment, and (5) store's value/price/status equation. Customers garner information from their friends, family, social networking sites, Internet videos, blogs, and their own experiences. They also share their experiences with their friends, family, and the world, often via the Internet. Finally, customers make their decisions based on all of this information. The challenge for retailers is to make the shopping experience desirable to the customer by developing the best possible shopping experience and then communicating the availability of this experience to the customer.

Retailers today face a difficult challenge in communicating with their customers in a way that inspires trust and engagement. In a world with social networking, blogs, and immediate news updates, retailers that do not respond quickly and honestly with customers will lose their customer base. One way that retailers hope to overcome the barrage of information, and become the retailer of choice, is through developing a program that offers insights into customer's behaviors, attitudes, and motivations. Retailers, vendors, and consultants spend both time and money trying to predict customers' behaviors based on a myriad of data. Once the data are collected, retailers hope to manipulate the shopping environment in their stores to serve the needs of their customers. This data is called shopping insights.

# Defining Shopper Insights

Win Weber pioneered category management with the Texas-based supermarket chain HEB. He defines shopper insights as "any insights necessary to understand the shopping experience including shopper need states, shopping occasions, shopper behavior in-store, drivers behind the purchase decision at the shelf and reaction patterns to particular in-store stimuli." Shopper insights enable retailers to assess/influence behavior at three activation points: (1) **shopper merchandising**, (2) **shopper marketing**, and (3) **consumer marketing**. Each activation point plays an important role in the total marketing mix. Shopper merchandising enhances the shopping experience through assortment and aligning the planogram with shopper needs. This includes the in-store drivers—aisle/department/store layout, visual displays, merchandising fixtures, and promotions. Shopper marketing uses marketing stimuli to build brand equity for the retailer and/or manufacturer brand. **Brand equity** includes all marketing outcomes accrued to a brand name compared to those accrued to a product without a name brand. Consumer marketing is all the pre-store communications and promotion, including product development, packaging, and advertisements.

Retailers seeking to effectively implement shopping insights need to: (1) develop and share a clear, actionable vision and strategy focused on shopper insights and shopper marketing; (2) align their insights about shoppers with the marketing functions within the organization; (3) reposition their category management, customer marketing, marketing, and consumer research functions; (4) design effective shopper research and shopper marketing strategies, and performance measures; and (5) encourage cross-functional collaboration within the retailer organization and with vendors. In sum, they need to review all aspects of the organizational effort to build the retailer's image through a careful examination that offers a fresh perspective of the retail organization.

# Common Retail Myths

One of the challenges in developing shopping insights is to begin by creating a fresh perspective. When seeking insights into shopping behavior, retailers must first eliminate preconceived ideas or myths about shoppers. The Hartman Group (THG) identified four common myths about shopping behavior:

1. **Brand loyalty drives shopping behavior.** Retailers and vendors typically believe that shoppers' **brand loyalty** drives their behavior. In reality, most shoppers plan their shopping experience around what they need, and where they should buy it, in the time frame their schedule allows or the **shopping occasion**. A decision tree is also useful in assessing how shoppers make decisions. These decisions forming the shopping occasion include: (1) Why must I shop? (2) Where are the products available? and (3) When can I shop? Some shopping occasions, such as for apparel and home furnishings, tend to focus more on brand loyalty, whereas shopping for other items—such as food, cleaning supplies, and home and garden supplies—are driven by efficiency and economy.

2. **Loyalty is built for CPG brands inside the store.** Many popular CPG brand vendors and retailers believe shoppers develop brand loyalty in the retail store. Instead, brand loyalty is driven by the individual's experience while consuming the brand. The memory of the consumption is the driving force. Brand loyalty is based on who the person was with, the activities involved, and the place of consumption. For instance, the pleasant memory of drinking a soft drink with a favorite grandparent, or the comfort of eating Vanilla Wafers in a banana pudding, makes the shopper associate a pleasant experience with a brand, thereby establishing brand loyalty.

3. **Shopping behavior is learned from parents or peers.** The way customers shop is based on the occasion, rather than the way their parents and peers shop. For instance, customers determine the mode of shopping by the importance they place on the product. When customers shop for products that identify them to others such as clothes, shoes, automobiles, purses, and homes, they use a more thoughtful approach to shopping. However, when a customer shops for products with little importance to themselves or others, they use a more efficient shopping mode.

4. **Customers are driven by the desire to purchase certain brands and products when shopping.** When shopping, customers are driven by the occasion. The shopping

experience is impacted by the customer's motivations for shopping, the intended recipient of the shopping experience, and their prior experiences. For instance, when shopping for a child's party, the parent's motivation may be to plan a party for 20 children at an economical price based on a baseball theme similar to that of the parent's childhood party experience. The experience is the driver of the shopping behavior, not the products or brands (Hartman 2004).

5. **Each of these myths have foundation in fact; however, the reality is slightly different.** Retailers must understand the drivers of shopping behavior in order to meet and exceed their expectations. The next step is to collect the necessary data in order to apply the reality of shoppers' behavior.

# Information Collection

To understand the drivers of shopping behavior, retailers collect information about shoppers. Many factors drive the shopping experience. To begin to understand shopping insights, two primary areas provide the basis for shopping insights: internal drivers and in-store drivers.

The **internal drivers** of shopping behavior focus on the shoppers' wants, needs, and behaviors. They are not directly influenced by the in-store environment and marketing. The internal drivers are:

1. Purpose of shopping trip or shopping occasion
2. Choosing retail store or channel that best meets the shoppers' needs
3. Level of brand loyalty by item, brand, and retailer
4. Perceptions and intended use of products or services
5. Shopper and consumer lifestyles
6. Shopping behavior or modes
7. Shopper's motivations

**In-store drivers** of shopping behavior include all aspects of the retail environment or atmosphere. This includes advertisements and promotions that the shopper experiences prior to entering the store. In-store drivers are:

1. Visual merchandising of the products
2. Store layout and design
3. Retail advertisements and promotion
4. Retail ambiance

Both internal and in-store drivers of shopping behavior are important to the overall experience. To determine desirable drivers for shoppers, retailers develop profiles of their best shopper groups. To develop a profile of potential customer(s), retailers and retail analysts typically use the following data collection methods:

1. **Observations:** Paco Underhill developed an extensive protocol for observing customer behavior. He and his staff videotape shoppers, and then analyze their behavior. Underhill noted several distinct behaviors caused by store design and visual merchandising techniques: Customers typically need to slow their walking speed to a shopping speed; during this shift in speed, customers do not see the full range of merchandise. Therefore,

place only a minimal amount of merchandise in this transition area. Female customers prefer tactile objects placed on tables rather than hangers. Therefore, when merchandising for female customers, place tactile objects where they are easily accessed. Because male customers, in general, shop quickly and do not like clutter, retailers should use fixtures that keep merchandise organized and not over-merchandise the men's area. Retailers also use security cameras to observe and record shopping behavior and track their paths through the shopping experience. Some shopping carts are equipped with sensors so that they may be tracked throughout the store to gain this information. Although the information gained from observations is valuable, it does not offer a complete picture into the shopping behavior of customers. Other methods of data collection make the picture of the shopping experience more complete.

2. **Intercept surveys:** Another method of collecting customer information is the intercept survey. Researchers or store employees stop customers while shopping or after they have completed their shopping experience, then ask a list of predetermined questions. They may also ask if they can inventory the items in their shopping cart or bag. This face-to-face method is effective in retrieving information about a particular shopping experience, as long as the shopper is comfortable sharing honestly with the employee or researcher.

3. **Pantry inventory:** Some research groups ask customers if they may visit their homes on a frequent basis and inventory their purchases. Other research groups, such as Nielsen, have a program whereby they carefully select a number of customers to represent a spectrum of American consumers. The participants are called panelists. Each panelist is given a home scanner; after they return from a shopping experience, they scan the bar code on all of the products they purchased. The panelists frequently upload the data from the scanner. This data collection method also offers rich data on a particular customer. The greater the number of panelists, the more likely the retailer or researcher can determine the likelihood that many shoppers shop in a similar manner. NPD Group (www.npd.com) and BigResearch (www.bigresearch.com) provide retailers and vendors with panel data. BigResearch uses an Internet-based panel to develop several products that retailers use to track shopping behavior and develop trends. They also track the type of media that shoppers use to find information.

4. **Focus groups:** A focus group is a data collection method whereby researchers invite selected customers to participate in a group interview session. Focus groups are usually audio-taped or video-taped. A moderator leads the participants in a series of questions developed to seek the information the researchers want. They are conducted in a room with a two-way mirror so that the retailer or vendor can watch the focus group as it progresses.

5. **Scanner data:** Retailers collect data during every transaction. The data collected is used in a number of ways. In category management, the data is used to perfect the merchandising set offered in each retail store by allowing the retailer to increase, decrease, or eliminate product facings. Retailers can also compare retail stores to determine whether a product offered in a similar store, but not offered in the other one, should be added to the merchandising set. Using scanner data, retailers can also begin to build a profile of customer market baskets. For instance, they may find that a customer who spends a lot of money buys staple products such as milk, eggs, meat, cereal, and vegetables. They can look at the basket and determine complementary products purchased together or particular brands they like. All of this information enables retailers to develop a profile of their customers and hopefully their shopping habits; however, this does not indicate the products they wanted but could not find, or that they purchase from other retailers. Scanner data

from multiple retailers is often compiled by companies such as Nielsen and the NPD Group to give retailers an overview of a single market. Nielsen Answers software, a recently introduced product, incorporates data from multiple sources into a graphic display of key performance indicators, allowing retailers and vendors to understand the status of a retailer or category at a glance. This software delivers the insights that enable category managers to immediately note areas that are growing or struggling. With today's vast amounts of data and fast pace, category managers must make decisions quickly—and a product such as Nielsen Answers simplifies the data mining process.

6. **Internet surveys:**  Many retailers now use online surveys to evaluate retail experiences. Surveys include a Web site and a coded number associated with the sales transaction; this number includes the following sales information: (1) time of day, (2) store location or number, (3) cashier, and (4) manager on duty.  The customer logs on to the Web site and uses this coded number to complete the survey. This type of survey is usually brief; however, many customers forgo the process unless they had an unusually bad or unusually good experience. Retailers, therefore, usually offer a potential incentive for the customer to complete the survey.  Common types of questions asked about the customer experience are: (1) store ambience (cleanliness, visual merchandising, store layout and design), (2) employee experience (friendliness and knowledge of employees), and (3) merchandise (price, value, and selection).

7. **Shopper segmentation techniques:**  Retailers and research companies use many techniques to segment shoppers based on lifestyle and demographic characteristics. Shoppers are classified by a number of criteria, including: (1) age, (2) race/ethnic group, (3) gender, (4) number of persons in household, (5) education, (6) income, and (7) zip code. The U.S. Census Bureau (www.census.gov) collects demographic data during the census period; many research companies use this information to develop a more in-depth profile by including lifestyle data.  Lifestyle data includes: (1) life stage, (2) interests, and (3) aspirations. Companies such as Nielsen Claritas  profile customers based on lifestyle and demographic data. The Claritas product, Prizm, segments customers by demographic and lifestyle data to enable retailers to develop shopping insights. One of the oldest segmentation strategies is Values, Attitudes, and Lifestyle (VALS), developed in the 1970s by SRI Consulting Business Intelligence. VALS segmented shoppers and gave each segment a name. One of the newest strategies is Lifestyles of Health and Sustainability, a market segment focused on health and fitness, the environment, personal development, sustainable living, and social justice. Although shoppers can be classified by demographic and lifestyle data, this doesn't tell the complete story of the shopper. Demographics and lifestyles sometimes change over time and sometimes quickly.

Each of these approaches is valuable and builds a profile of the shopper. However, a global approach using a combination of approaches will build a more complete profile, leading the retailer to develop true shopping insights. In addition, collecting data to define the shopper, to determine the mode of shopping is important.

# Shopping Modes

Shoppers have several modes when shopping, depending on the product, brand loyalty, time and money. One of the challenges for retailers and brand managers is that 70% of all purchase decisions are made standing in front of the shelf. This means the insights on how a person shops a category is extremely important. Further, the implication for a category manager becomes one of assuring the right amount of product is in the right place at the right time with the right signage, advertisements, or promotions. Nielsen has identified four different mindsets of shoppers:

1. **Auto-pilot mode:** when customers make decisions based on brand choices. These decisions are usually habitual, where they simply "grab and go." Shoppers are somewhat indifferent to the brand and likely to switch brands if the product is out of stock. Typical items are: coffee, cheese, butter, bottled water, mayonnaise, nuts, soft drinks, and detergent.

2. **Experimental or variety seeking or browser mode:** when customers browse the shelves looking for new or different products. They are looking for a new taste experience or interesting new products. Typical items are: cookies, salad dressing, chewing gum, breakfast bars, frozen snacks, cold cereal, and frozen dinners or entrées.

3. **Buzz mode:** when customers make their purchase decisions based on new advertisements, innovative packaging, or promotions. Typical items are: ready-to-drink teas, smoothies and yogurt drinks, sports and energy drinks, and chocolate.

4. **Bargain-hunting mode:** when customers make decisions based on price comparison and promotions. This customer is motivated by saving money. Typical items are: canned tuna, canned tomatoes, canned fruit, and pasta sauce.

Every shopper falls into one or more of these modes at some time during any number of shopping experiences. Internal in-store drivers of shopping behavior all become merged during these modes. Demographics and lifestyles remain important, but any shopper from any segment can fall into these behaviors, depending on the shopping mission. In the past, retailers focused on a silo mentality to meet customer needs and to gain market advantage. A silo mentality is one in which the retailer focuses on a very narrow aspect of a challenge and does not assess outside factors that may impact the market or customer. As shopper insights became important to retailers, category management developed a new perspective to include these insights.

# Shopper and Category Management

Retailers now focus on both the logistics/efficiency required to enhance the shopping experience and shopper behavior. The newest category management process described by Brian Harris of the Partnering Group includes shopping insights. This shopper-centric model includes: category definition, category role, insight generation, strategic and tactical planning, initiative development, plan launch, and category review. Although very similar to the older model, it takes into account the shopper and includes information gathered through loyalty programs. The new model is a seven-step cycle (see Figure 9.1), with several steps common to the old cycle. Category definition and category role are still important, and form the basis for category development. However, there is now a greater focus on alignment with the overall retail strategy and the destination categories. This step is now performed only when necessary, thus shortening the cycle. The heart of the new cycle is: (1) plan review, (2) insight generation, (3) strategic planning, (4) tactical planning, (5) initiative development, (6) plan launch, and (7) plan

FIGURE 9.1 *New Category Cycle* (Courtesy of The Partnering Group)

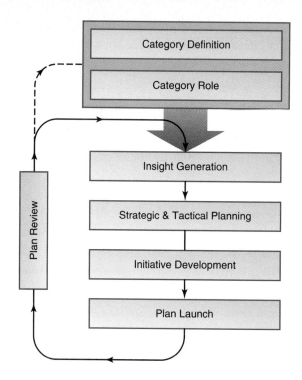

review. There is greater focus on finding key opportunities within a category, and a greater understanding of both shopper behavior and the answer to the key business question: how to serve the customer while improving the bottom line.

During insight generation, retailers review the current retail environment by assessing key business questions related to: (1) consumers and shoppers, (2) products and services, (3) overall retail market, (4) retailer and direct competitors, and (5) shopper loyalty. The process includes all of the steps typical to market research: reviewing the current status, developing hypotheses or questions, and analyzing data—which ultimate provide the insights into shoppers' behavior. When incorporating shopper insights into category management, retailers can begin to plan their assortment and merchandising by the way the customer shops. For instance, customers may be overwhelmed by the selection. Retailers can analyze the POS data to spot trends to determine the best assortment for a given category by eliminating choices.

In the new cycle, strategies and tactics are more integrated, with a greater focus on the consumer and shopper. Strategies focus on the differences between other retailers, whereas tactics focus on planning for the category on a local basis. The five new strategies are: (1) conversion, (2) transaction, (3) enthusiast, (4) consumption, and (5) shopper segment. The conversion strategy aims to bring the shopper to the point of buying by making the category easy to shop. The transaction strategy is designed to encourage the shopper to trade up by buying larger sizes or larger quantities within a category. This strategy is also designed to cross-merchandise within a category, thereby building total sales and profit. The enthusiast strategy focuses on the brand-loyal or enthusiastic shopper. These shoppers purchase a number of products offered by a favored brand and are not driven by price. To encourage this shopper, retailers focus on target marketing strategies. The consumption strategy focuses on encouraging shoppers to try a new product, and is usually an occasion-based buying decision. The final strategy is the shopper-segment strategy; retailers focus on targeting a specific segment. This strategy is an important source of sales, profit, and image to the retailer and allows vendors to develop a new, emerging shopper base.

Within this strategy/tactics integration, retailers and vendors should link the two. When deciding on the strategy for a category, retailers relate the objective of the strategy, products in the category, and the manner in which retailers evaluate the category to the tactic. The tactics will be refined on the local level.

Once the strategies and tactics are determined and linked, the retailer develops the initiative that precedes the category launch. The goal is to develop differentiating and sustainable category initiatives while implementing rigorous cost/benefit analyses and prioritizing categories and brands. This step is important because it enables retailers to deliver differentiation and innovation to a category plan, and focus on implementation which will eventually be evaluated by the scorecard.

The Plan Launch includes a detailed implementation plan tied to each initiative, a formal approval and executive commitment process, and allows the retailer to set an achievable score card target. The improved scorecard target setting enables retailers to measure the success of the category more accurately (The Partnering Group 2009).

# Review

This chapter focused on the development of shopper insights and the new category management cycle developed by the Partnering Group in 2009 for the Food Marketing Institute. Customers have opinions and can now share these opinions about every facet of the retail experience, including the (1) store's physical environment and location, (2) employee's knowledge level and attitudes, (3) quality and quantity of the store's product assortment, (4) store's commitment to the environment, and (5) store's value/price/status equation. Win Weber defines shopper insights as "any insights necessary to understand the shopping experience including shopper need states, shopping occasions, shopper behavior in-store, drivers behind the purchase decision at the shelf and reaction patterns to particular in-store stimuli." Retailers seeking to effectively implement shopping insights need to: (1) develop and share a clear, actionable vision and strategy focused on shopper insights and shopper marketing; (2) align their insights about shoppers with the marketing functions within the organization; (3) reposition their category management, customer marketing, marketing, and consumer research functions; (4) design effective shopper research and shopper marketing strategies and performance measures, and (5) encourage cross-functional collaboration within the retailer organization and with vendors.

Retailers must determine the realities driving shopper behavior, collect data about shopping behavior by a number of methodologies, and respond to the modes of shopping in order to best serve the shopper. One of initiatives to encompass this information and provide better service is the newest category management process described by Brian Harris of the Partnering Group for the Food Marketing Institute. This shopper-centric model includes: category definition, category role, insight generation, strategic and tactical planning, initiative development, plan launch, and category review. Although very similar to the older model, this model takes in account the shopper and includes information gathered through loyalty programs.

# key terms

Auto-pilot mode   103

Bargain-hunting mode   103

Brand equity   98

Brand loyalty   99

Browser mode   103

Buzz mode   103

Consumer marketing   98

Focus groups   101

In-store drivers   100

Intercept surveys   101

Internal drivers   100

Internet surveys   102

Pantry inventory   101

Scanner data   101

Shopper insights   98

Shopper marketing   98

Shopper merchandising   98

Shopper segmentations   102

Shopping modes   102

# activities

- From the category chosen in Chapter 5:
  - Analyze how the retailer has merchandised each, including, but not limited to:
    - Products
    - Brands, including private label
    - Brand extensions
    - Placement, including shelf height from floor, left to right, etc.
    - Adjacent product placements
    - Number of facings

- Assess the strengths and weaknesses of each merchandising set.
- What assumptions can you make in regard to shopper insights by your analysis?
- What recommendations would you make to the retailer in regard to their categories?
- Do you believe they have accurately served their customers?

# discussion questions

1. Explain how the concept of shopper insights changed retailing.
2. List the facets of the retail experience.
3. Cite the modes of communication between the retailer and shopper.
4. Explain the three activation points of retailers and shoppers.
5. Identify the myths of retailing with the reality of shopper behavior.
6. Differentiate between the internal drivers and the in-store drivers of shopping behavior.
7. Summarize the data collection techniques that retailers use.
8. Differentiate the shopper segmentation strategies.
9. Compare the four different modes of shopping.
10. Compare the new category management cycle with the old cycle.
11. Evaluate the benefits of including shopper insights.
12. Draw the new category management cycle.

# references, resources, web sites, and recommended readings

- Lifestyles of Health and Sustainability. http://www.lohas.com/
- Hartman Group. 2004. *Defining shopper insights: Our framework of understanding*. Bellevue, Washington: The Hartman Group.
- Hartman Group. 2005. *Extending shopper insights: Understanding cultural dynamics*. Bellevue, Washington: The Hartman Group.
- Nielsen. http://www.nielsen.com/
- Nielsen Claritas. http://www.claritas.com/
- The Partnering Group. 2009. *Shopper and category development: The next generation of best practices*. Food Marketing Institute (In press).
- Underhill, P. 2000. *Why we buy: The science of shopping*. New York: Simon and Schuster.

# CAREERS IN CATEGORY MANAGEMENT

**LEARNING GOALS**

On completion of this chapter, the student will be able to:

- List the job titles common to space management and category management.
- Identify avenues to locating positions in space management and category management.
- Give examples of skills that employers seek.
- Discuss the typical activities of a space manager or category manager.
- Explain the importance of teamwork.
- Differentiate the types of panel interviews.
- Plan a strategy for the job application process.
- Discuss the abilities needed for certification standards.

10

# Introduction

There are many career opportunities in the retail industry. Technology-related careers in retail, such as **space management** and category management, are becoming increasingly popular throughout the world. The titles of the positions vary by organization and country; however, the skill set for success is similar. Table 10.1 lists many of the common job titles. This chapter focuses on preparing for a career in space and category management.

## TABLE 10.1

### Commonly Used Titles Directly Related to Category Management According to the Category Management Association

| | |
|---|---|
| Assistant Category Manager | Category Management Sales Technology |
| Associate Category Management Manager | |
| Associate Category Manager | Category Management Systems Manager |
| Associate Director Consumer Insights | |
| Brand & Category Development Manager | Category Manager |
| Business Analyst | Category Planning Manager |
| Business Analyst Supervisor | Category Research & Analysis Manager |
| Business Development Category Analyst | Category Retail Planning Analyst |
| Business Information Manager | Category Sales Manager |
| Business Marketing Analyst | Category Sales Planner |
| Business Planner, IT | Category Sales Research Manager |
| Category Advisor | Category Specialist |
| Category Advisor Manager | Category Strategy Manager |
| Category Analyst | Category Team Leader |
| Category Analyst II | Category Trade Manager |
| Category Business Analyst | Category Trade Marketing Manager |
| Category Business Director | Category/Space Management Specialist |
| Category Development Analyst | |
| Category Development and Shopper Insights Manager | Chain Sales Analyst |
| | Channel Planning Manager |
| Category Development Associate | Consumer Insights Manager |
| Category Development Manager | Consumer Research & Analysis Manager |
| Category Director | |
| Category Information Manager | Customer Category Management |
| Category Insights Manager | Customer Category Manager II |
| Category Leadership Manager | Customer Development Insights Manager |
| Category Management | |
| Category Management Analyst | Customer Insights Manager |
| Category Management Assistant | Customer Marketing & Category Management |
| Category Management Insights Marketing Manager | |
| | Customer Marketing Manager |

*(continued)*

TABLE 10.1

**(continued)**

| | |
|---|---|
| Customer Trade Marketing Manager | Sales and Marketing Analyst |
| Inventory Sales Analyst | Sales and Marketing Decision Support Analyst |
| Junior Category Manager/Category Analyst | Sales Planning and Development Manager |
| Market Insights Manager | Sales Planning Director |
| Merchandising Manager | Sales Planning Manager |
| Modular Analyst | Sales Pricing Analyst |
| Planogram Manager | Sales Strategy Manager |
| Replenishment Manager | Shelf Analyst |
| Retail Information Manager | Shopper Insights Manager |
| Retail Space Specialist | Space Management Analyst |
| Sales & Category Analyst | Space Management Coordinator |
| Sales & Marketing Manager Analyst | Space Manager |
| Sales & Marketing System Manager | Space Planner |
| | Space Planning Manager |
| Sales Analyst | Trade Analyst |
| Sales Analyst, Customer Marketing | Trade Marketing Analyst |
| | Trade Marketing Manager |

# Career Search

There are several avenues to locating positions in space management and category management, including: (1) searching for positions on career Web sites such as monster.com and careerbuilder.com; (2) campus recruitment activities and **career fairs**; (3) professional organizations such as the Category Management Association; (4) **networking** with professionals in the field; (5) joining networking sites like Linkedin.com, which has groups specific to the category management industry; (6) attending professional or industry meetings like JDA Focus, The Council of Supply Chain Management Professionals, Category Management Association Conference, The Association for Operations Management Conference and Expo, National Retail Federation (NRF) Meeting, Retail Industry Leaders Association (RILA) Meeting; and (7) participating in postgraduate training programs such as Nielsen's Emerging Leaders Program. All of these avenues provide you with opportunities to learn about a career in space and category management. Attending meetings gives you opportunities to network with professionals in the field as well as meet recruiters. Table 10.2 is an example of a job announcement for a category management position.

TABLE 10.2

| Sample Advertisement for a Category Manager |
| --- |

**Position:**

- Responsible for driving category leadership role
- Provide analytical expertise and project leadership
- Provide shopper insights
- Understand current industry trends
- Identify future opportunities
- Monitor market and retail competitors
- Analyze and identify category, segment, and brand performance opportunities

**Qualifications:**

- Bachelor's degree
- Strong technical skills
- Advanced Microsoft Office Suite ability with database reporting skills
- Experience analyzing and applying consumer research
- Experience with IRI, ACNielsen, or NDP data
- Space management software skills (Space Planning or Spaceman)
- Independent worker who is also a team player

# Employee Skills

The goal of any employer, when hiring a new employee, is finding one who will become a success within the organization, add value to the organization, and want to stay with the organization. There are many universal skills that employers seek in new employees. These skills include, but are not limited to: (1) intellect; (2) academic performance; (3) **extracurricular activities**; (4) relevant job experience; (5) enthusiasm for seeking a position with a company; (6) ability to lead/manage others; (7) good communication skills, both verbal and written; (8) problem-solving skills; (9) teamwork; and (10) a personality that is compatible with the organization's culture. In addition to these skills, retailers seeking employees for retail technology positions look for: (1) computer skills, (2) **analytical skills**, (3) self-motivation, (4) willingness to learn, (5) good presentation skills, (6) an understanding of **shopper insights**, and (8) understanding and previous use of syndicated data or panel data.

Most recruiters assume that recent college graduates are proficient in Microsoft Word and Microsoft PowerPoint; however, in retail technology they also expect students to be proficient in Microsoft Excel and desire applicants to be proficient in Microsoft Access. Retailers may also seek applicants with skill using any one of a number of industry software packages, including JDA Space Planning™, JDA Floor Planning™, ACNielsen Spaceman™, or IRI Apollo™. A portfolio of work is an excellent tool to exhibit projects using these software packages.

In category management, having good analytical skills is extremely important. Retailers want candidates to understand the importance of data analysis in making decisions about every aspect of space management, category management, and store layout and design. For instance, the retailer expects the employee to review POS data to determine trends within a category, segment, subsegment, and brand. These decisions will lead to increasing or decreasing space on a shelf or in the store. A category of merchandise that is performing poorly may be given a smaller area in a store, whereas another category that is performing better than expected is given a larger space. The employee is expected to explain why the change should be made, make projections about future sales in both areas, and present the information in both a concise yet fact-filled presentation. In addition to analyzing the POS data, employees are also expected to review and analyze syndicated data to determine if there are evolving trends that will increase opportunities for sales for the retailer, or identify current sales trends in which the competitors are successful and the retailer is currently not competitive.

Although most corporate positions are team based, the prospective employee must also be self-motivated. Each category manager or space manager has an area of emphasis with a level of responsibility. Although a supervisor may give the employee a time frame to complete a project, a successful employee must be able to manage their time well, set goals for themselves, and reach the goals with little or no supervision. An employee may be on a number of teams and report to a number of supervisors. Some teams will be within a department, others will be cross-functional teams. For instance, a category manager may be on a team with buyers, store layout and design team members, and real estate team members. When working with teams, the ability to negotiate becomes very important. Although everyone must at sometime make concessions, they must also be able to present their view in a persuasive manner.

# Résumé

The first step in preparing for an interview is preparing a good **résumé**. A good résumé for a recent college graduate is in **reverse chronological order**, accurate, easy to ready, and one page. The résumé sent to a given employer focuses on the skills a student has in relationship to the skills the employer seeks. For instance, retailers will look for: (1) relevant job experience, (2) relevant coursework, (3) and extracurricular activities. In addition, during the interview, they will ask leading questions to determine your knowledge, skills, talents, personality characteristics, values, and social skills. The interview may be one recruiter with one candidate or one of three types of **panel interviews**: (1) one recruiter with multiple candidates, (2) more than one recruiter with one candidate, or (3) multiple recruiters and multiple candidates. One of the challenges in a panel interview with multiple candidates is to ensure that the other candidates do not monopolize the interview. In this situation, the recruiters are able to compare the candidates' knowledge and personalities at one time in a stressful situation. Nonverbal language, including good eye contact, is important in all interview formats, but particularly important when there a number of people involved. In a panel interview, the applicant should give a copy of their résumé to each panel member.

# Interviews

An interview is the first opportunity that a prospective employee has to assess a candidate's personality and ability to communicate effectively. Many recruiters use a scale to rate the responses of each candidate, and then rank all of the candidates in all types of interviews. If the candidate is ranked highly by the recruiter in relationship to the other candidates, the recruiter will ask the candidate to proceed further in the interview process.

Many employers now use a **telephone interview** to screen potential candidates. During the telephone interview a recruiter generally asks a series of prepared questions of each potential candidate. This interview is completely **depersonalized**; the recruiter may even tell the applicant they can only repeat the questions, they may not reword or explain the questions. An applicant should prepare for this interview as with the other types of interviews. In preparation for an interview, the applicant should be having: a copy of the résumé, the **job description**, and a list of potential questions for the recruiter. Although the recruiter may say the interview will last only a given period of time, allow more time for the interview because the recruiter may call earlier or later than scheduled. One of the most important considerations during a telephone interview is for the applicant to choose their location during the call wisely, one in which there will be no interruptions or disturbances.

Another type is the personal interview, in which the recruiter and candidate are in a traditional interview setting. The recruiter may interview in a college campus career office, a local or regional office, or ask the candidate to travel to the corporate office for an interview. Many retailers require candidates to complete a screening exam prior to the interview. This exam may include retail math and a demonstration of software skills, particularly Microsoft Excel. Many retailers also check the credit rating of candidates as well as require a drug test.

Most positions in space management and category management are corporate level; therefore, the final candidates often interview at the corporate office. Corporate interviews usually include a series of interviews and one or more meal functions. The expense of hiring and training a new employee necessitates learning as much as possible about a potential employee. This includes everything from their attire, behavior, table manners, and even checking their consumption of alcohol and the ensuing behavior. Interviews also include questions related to technology skills. For instance, many retailers ask students to rate their skill in using Microsoft Excel or Microsoft Access. The question is often worded like this, "On a scale of 1 to 10, with 10 being able to write macros in Excel; how would you rate your skill in Excel?" It is important that candidates do not exaggerate their level of skills in this situation, because the interviewer may have follow-up questions for different levels of responses from the candidates.

# Follow-up

After students have completed an interview, a thank-you note reminding the recruiter of the student's interest in the position should be written. Although many candidates write thank-you emails, a handwritten note is more formal and often more impressive. A recruiter generally tells candidates that they will hear from the recruiter within a stated period of time. A recruiter will contact those fitting the criteria best more quickly than those who do not.

# Guidelines for Success

The following is a universal list of guidelines for success. These guidelines are useful in any occupation in any setting. A successful employee incorporates these into their everyday work life. This code enables you to comply with the organization's culture while achieving personal success.

1. **Set goals for yourself:** Research has found that individuals who set goals for themselves often feel obligated, and thus, more likely to complete or accomplish them.

2. **Take advantage of training opportunities:** Most companies offer continuing education or training classes in addition to the required training for new employees. These classes often provide you with the necessary skills you need to "move-up" the career ladder to your next position. Supervisors often look to individuals who have completed training to move them to the next job level.

3. **Find a mentor:** Employees who have been with the company for a while often are the best people to tap as a mentor. They can show the new people "how to get things done" or even just introduce them to other employees in the company.

4. **Read trade publications:** Reading trade publications often provides you with the current trends and research in your industry.

5. **Read internal publications:** Reading internal publications provides you with information related to your own organization. For example, the company may announce its expansion plan in the internal newsletter; you may then be able ask your supervisor to be considered for a new position in the new stores.

6. **Join professional organizations:** Joining professional organizations provides you with the opportunity to network with people in your field, especially during their annual conventions or meetings. Newsletters or bulletins from these organizations often provide up-to-date information regarding the industry.

7. **Learn the company culture and play by the rules:** Learning the company culture gives you a better understanding of how "things work" inside the organization.

8. **Make work-friends wisely (do not befriend complainers and gossipers):** Choosing your friends wisely inside your work organization will add to your success by providing a positive support group.

9. **Develop a code of ethics:** An ethical employee seeks to always perform his/her job well and makes ethical decisions even when an unethical decision would be easier or seemingly unnoticed.

# Certification Standards

In addition to a code for success, a common standard indicating skill and knowledge sets allows you to determine your strengths and weaknesses. The Category Management Standards and Certification Steering Committee was formed to address opportunities and gaps pertaining to industry guidelines and skill set definitions for category management professionals. Contributors to the standards represented many companies and universities, including: Abbott Nutrition, Anheuser-Busch, Coca-Cola Enterprises, Coca-Cola North America, Colgate Palmolive, Del Monte, DePaul University, Dr. Pepper Snapple Group, EJ Gallo, Hormel Foods, Johnson & Johnson, Johnson Controls, Kellogg, Nestle Purina, St. Joseph's University, Swedish Match,

University of Pittsburgh, Western Michigan University, and Wrigley. The committee developed guidelines and skill set definitions for category management professionals. Their mission was to provide the category management industry with three key deliverables:

1. General guidelines for manufacturers' category management organizational structure and roles.
2. Definition of skill proficiency expected in category management roles.
3. Certification of training programs that conform to the standards established by the committee, with sufficient rigor to merit the endorsement.

Table 10.3 includes the roles within the category management team, with a general description of the work and typical skill sets required. Space management and category management professionals now have a matrix by which they can determine the skills and knowledge sets they need to improve upon in order to progress through an organization. Certification recognizes individuals for specific skill mastery, and provides incentives for all category and space management professionals to pursue higher levels of performance and certification.

Category and space management is a relatively new field in the retailing industry. As technological applications improve and change, category and space management will also change. However, the knowledge and skills translate to other avenues in the corporate retail environment. When choosing an employer, look for one that values your knowledge and skills and gives you opportunities to move within the organization. Most corporate teams are cross-functional. This allows employees to learn about other areas and determine their career paths.

# Review

Retail technology offers many career opportunities, particularly in space management and category management, throughout the world. There are many avenues to learning about positions in the field, including professional organizations, professional meetings, and career Web sites. Employers seek many universal skills in new employees; however, this field also has expectations in regard to software and analytical skills.

The first step in getting ready for an interview is preparing a good résumé. A good résumé for a recent college graduate is in reverse chronological order, accurate, easy to read, and one page. The résumé sent to a potential employer focuses on the skills a student has in relationship to the skills the employer seeks. An interview is the first opportunity that a prospective employee has to assess a candidate's personality and ability to communicate effectively. After students have completed an interview, a thank-you note reminding the recruiter of the student's interest in the position should be written. A successful employee in any organization develops a code by which they work. This code enables them to comply with the organization's culture while achieving personal success. In addition to a code for success, a common standard indicating skill and knowledge sets allows you to determine your strengths and weaknesses. The Category Management Standards and Certification Steering Committee developed guidelines and skill set definitions for category management professionals. Category and space management is a relatively new field in the retailing industry. As technological applications improve and change, category and space management will also change. However, the knowledge and skills translate to other avenues in the corporate retail environment.

TABLE 10.3

## Category Management Team (Courtesy of the Category Management Association)

| Learning Programs by Level | Certified Professional Category Analyst CPCA | Certified Professional Category Manager CPCM | Certified Professional Strategic Advisor CPSA |
|---|---|---|---|
| Email, Calendar, Task, & Content Mgmt Software | Recommended | | |
| Word Processing Software | Recommended | | |
| Basic Industry Knowledge | REQUIRED | | |
| Category Management History and Process | REQUIRED | | |
| Pricing Analysis | REQUIRED | | |
| Promotion Analysis | REQUIRED | | |
| Assortment Analysis | REQUIRED | REQUIRED | |
| Spreadsheet Development Software | REQUIRED | REQUIRED | |
| Presentation Development Software | REQUIRED | REQUIRED | |
| Space Planning Software | REQUIRED | REQUIRED | |
| Syndicated Data Software | REQUIRED | REQUIRED | |
| Syndicated Panel Software Relational Databases | REQUIRED | REQUIRED | |
| Recommended | Recommended | Recommended | |
| Presenting Effectively | | Recommended | |
| Ethical Expectations and Legal Implications | | Recommended | |
| Syndicated Store-Level Data & Retailer POS Data Analysis | | REQUIRED | |
| Syndicated Spectra Software | | REQUIRED | |
| Opportunity Identification for Actionable Insights | | REQUIRED | |
| Root Cause Analytics | | REQUIRED | |
| Comprehensive Category Reviews | | REQUIRED | |
| Understanding Category Shopper Behavior | | REQUIRED | |
| Leveraging Data for Basic Business Solutions | | REQUIRED | |
| Retailer Economics and Supply Chain | | REQUIRED | REQUIRED |
| Customer Relationship Management Software | | Recommended | Recommended |
| Joint Business Planning & Value Creation | | | REQUIRED |
| Collaborative Partnerships | | | REQUIRED |
| Consultative Selling | | | REQUIRED |
| Understanding Shopper Behavior Beyond the Category | | | REQUIRED |
| Retailer Shopper Segmentation | | | REQUIRED |
| Leveraging Data for Advanced Shelving Solutions | | | REQUIRED |
| Leveraging Data for Advanced Assortment Solutions | | | REQUIRED |
| Advanced Pricing Analysis | | | Recommended |
| Advanced Promotion Analysis | | | Recommended |

# key terms

# activities

- Search job Web sites for category management and space management positions.
- Search the Web for résumé writing skills.
- Search the Web for interview skill sites.
- Set up mock interviews with the college career center.
- Ask a group of friends to participate in a mock panel interview.

# discussion questions

1. How does your background and skill set position you for a job in category management?

2. How do you plan to improve upon your existing knowledge and skills to become a top candidate for a position in category management?

3. On a scale of 1 to 10 with 10 representing writing macros, what is your skill level in Excel? Justify your answer.

4. Give examples of when you worked on a team and had to convince others to your point of view.

5. Give an example of a time when you believed the team needed a leader and you stepped up.

6. Explain how you would prepare for a panel interview.

7. What are typical questions you would ask a recruiter during an interview?

8. Why do you think certification in category management is important?

# references, resources, web sites, and recommended readings

- ACNielsen. http://www.nielsen.com/
- Careerbuilder. http://www.careerbuilder.com/
- Category Management Association. http://www.cpgcatnet.org/
- Council of Supply Chain Management Associations. http://www.cscmp.org/
- Information Resources, Inc. (IRI). http://www.us.infores.com/
- JDA Software. http://www.jda.com/
- Monster. http://www.monster.com/
- National Retail Federation. http://www.nrf.com/
- Retail Industry Leaders Association. http://www.rila.org/

# Index